Christopher Gist

Frontier Scout

Allan Powell

Hagerstown, Maryland

1992

This Burd Street Press publication
was printed by
Beidel Printing House, Inc.
63 West Burd Street
Shippensburg, PA 17257 USA

ISBN 0-942597-50-8

In respect for the scholarship contained herein, the acid-free paper used in this book
meets the guidelines for permanence and durability of the Committee on Production
Guidelines for Book Longevity of the Council on Library Resources.

For a complete list of available publications
please write
Burd Street Press
Division of White Mane Publishing Company, Inc.
P.O. Box 152
Shippensburg, PA 17257 USA

PRINTED IN THE UNITED STATES OF AMERICA

<u>Our</u> <u>Thanks</u>

Joanie Powell - For her steadfast support during the many details of
producing this book.

Dr. Harold Gist - For encouragement in writing about one of the lesser known
but great Maryland heroes.

About the Cover Picture
Gist and Washington at Fort Le Boeuf
origin unknown
Presented to author by Dr. William C. Gist
of Louisville, Kentucky. He is an eighth
generation nephew of Christopher Gist.

FOREWORD

While doing extensive reading on the French and Indian War period of American history, I became aware of the unusual experiences of Christopher Gist. Yet he did not seem to catch the attention given to other scouts, traders and frontiersmen of the time.

It is hard to measure the importance of Christopher Gist in the larger picture of frontier development, but it has been my growing opinion that he has been neglected and that he deserves recognition that has so far not been given.

Hopefully, this small work will be a contribution to any efforts to give this heroic figure a more prominent place in history.

Allan Powell
Hagerstown, Md.

TABLE OF CONTENTS

Chapter I

From Baltimore Town to the Wilderness Trail

"Sunday 18 - I was very sick, and sweated myself according to the Indian Custom in a Sweat-House, which gave Me Ease and my Fever abated."[1] So wrote Christopher Gist in his Journal for November 18, 1750 while on the trail to Loyalhannan, an Indian village at the present site of Ft. Ligonier.

This was only the beginning of many aches and pains which would rack his trail worn body. Ahead lay only foot trails used by Indian warriors and traders with their pack horses. The worst of the winter season was yet to come. The perils of ice and snow--bad as they were--might be no equal to the perils of dealing with the Indians who looked with suspicion on the increasing numbers of white settlers.

As the steam worked its beneficial powers through his feverish body, Christopher's mind wandered back to earlier times around Baltimore Town when family and friends were nearby. The well-stocked plantation of his boyhood seemed like a figment of his imagination. So much had changed that he wondered if he were merely imagining this affluent past. At forty-five and on a barren, moccasin-packed trail with only his black, seventeen-year-old servant, Christopher might well have had self-doubt about the journey he was taking. But he was now committed to the task ahead. To back out would make it appear that he was afraid of the rigors of the forest. Property, family, neighbors, townspeople and the hub-bub of society were now well behind, and only miles of leafless woods lay ahead.

Even the pleasing vapors of the steam could not keep his memory from jogging back to others who had faced danger to discover new lands. His grandfather, Christopher Gist, along with his grandmother, Edith, had braved the treacherous Atlantic when they migrated from England to the Province of Maryland before 1679 to settle in Baltimore County. The Gist family had a long and distinguished history in England.

> The name "Gist" is variously spelled in the records of the family. It assumes the forms "Guest," "Gest," "Geyste," "Ghest," "le Gest," "le Gist," and "Gist". . . . Gist is said to signify "the guest, the received stranger."[2]

---

[1] William M. Darlington, <u>Christopher Gist's Journals</u>, P. 33. (Hereafter referred to as <u>Journals</u> and means #1).

[2] Wilson Gee, <u>The Gist Family of South Carolina and Its Maryland Antecedents</u>, p. 1.

Starting with 150 acres of land, his industry was soon rewarded with another 245.[3] This was only the beginning. He soon became a prosperous planter with a riverfront wharf necessary for shipping produce to England and for receiving goods not yet produced in the colonies.

As a man of property, the elder Gist served as a member of the Grand Jury for several years. In 1689 he was commissioned as a Justice of Baltimore County. His life of hard work and service came to an end in 1690 after only eleven years in the new land. In his will he declared,

> I Christopher Guest[4] of Baltimore County being weak in body--but of good and perfect memory--thanks to G. and calling to membrance the uncertain estate of this transitory life and that all of us must yield unto death, when it shall please God to call--do make constitute fordaine and declare this my L. W. & T. -- therefore I give my dearly beloved wife full power to receive all debts owing to her and likewise to pay all debts--and being paid I give her full power to dispose of all my lands and goods. . . .[5]

Edith Gist took care that their only son, Richard, was to be secure not only in worldly goods but that he was also properly educated. When she died in 1694, her will provided that her brother, Richard Cromwell and a Mr. Thomas Staley take ". . . into their custody and tutelage my son Richard Gist who I request may be put to school and there kept till he can wright and cost accompt fitting for merchant business.[6]

Richard Gist, the father of Christopher Gist who was to achieve fame as a guide, scout surveyor, explorer and soldier, was only seven years old when his father died. The will provided that he inherit a negro servant at the age of sixteen. In 1693 he also became the owner of a tract of land of 225 acres called "Gist's Rest."

Young Richard lived with his uncle, Richard Cromwell, who had a store in his plantation home. Here he learned the basics of business. Accounting and trading were routine activity for business interests along the Patapsco River. As Richard applied himself, he too prospered and added to his inheritance.

When he became twenty-one, Richard married Zipporah Murray. Their marriage resulted in nine children--five boys and four girls. The oldest of the children, Christopher, was expected to continue the family tradition of

---

[3] Jean Muir Dorsey and Maxwell Jay Dorsey, Christopher Gist of Maryland and Some of His Descendants, P. 1. An excellent source for records of the Gist family land holdings.

[4] Different spellings may indicate spelling errors by the clerk. But, as has been noted, the "Gist" name has been spelled variously.

[5] Ibid. P. 1.

[6] Christopher Johnston, "Gist Family of Baltimore County," Maryland Historical Magazine, December 1913, P. 373.

acquiring land and expanding business as his father was then doing. Meanwhile, Richard acquired "Turkey Cock Hall" comprising 200 acres. Then came "Adventure" composed of 725 acres and "Green Spring Traverse" made up of 300 acres. The new world was good to the elder Gist and his son.

But there is more to tell. In addition to being a planter and merchant, Richard Gist helped in the grueling work of laying out and clearing roads. It is very likely that some of his business was done in Baltimore Town after the town was laid out.

Richard Gist was clearly a man of many talents. He was appointed one of the Justices of Baltimore County--eventually becoming presiding Justice. He also represented his county in the Provincial Assembly. His knowledge of surveying made him useful in helping to lay out the town of Baltimore and later to become deputy surveyor of the Western Shore of Maryland.[7] When he died in 1741, Richard Gist left no will. Since Christopher was the oldest son, it is probable that he inherited most of his father's estate. But something else in the Gist household must have lead to this result. In 1724, seventeen years before his death, Richard Gist placed this notice before the public.

> This is to certify and give Notice to All Persons Whatsoever that I Richard Gist of Baltimore County doe forwarne all manner of persons Whatsoever to have any dealings with my wife Zipporah Gist to take or receive any Thing Whatsoever upon pretence Whatever That is belonging to me or in any wise Whatever kind if that person Shall persume to doe that it be their own Peril given under my hand this Aug. 1724.[8]

Whatever the reason for this public notice, it would contribute toward making the oldest son, Christopher, the prime beneficiary of the father's estate.

Surprisingly little is known about Christopher's early life. There is disagreement even about his birth date. Some say he was born c. 1705 while others report c. 1706. But he, like other children, was expected to help in the many duties that made up the daily life of a planter-mercantile family. Christopher undoubtedly helped around the plantation near Baltimore Town and he must have taken a fancy to the surveying instruments used by his father.

There is reason to believe Christopher had some business sense because he added to what he inherited by buying lot #56 in Baltimore Town on a tract of 500 acres called "Joshua's Lot" in Baltimore County.[9] Other land purchases

---

[7] Jean Muir Dorsey and Maxwell Jay Dorsey, Op.Cit., p. 7.

[8] Ibid., p. 8.

[9] Ibid., p. 11.

followed. Then too, he helped survey and clear roads in Baltimore County--
becoming overseer in 1734.

Life must have been varied and interesting for Christopher. It is
reported that he "received money for the heads of four wolves he had
killed."[10] And strange as it may seem, he obtained a commission in 1743 as
Coroner in Baltimore County.[11] Apparently Christopher would try anything
once.

In due time (about 1742) Christopher wanted to try his hand as a
merchant. He was now thirty-seven years old but still ready for new
adventure. Things must have gone well in the early stages of the venture
because he purchased a sloop of about forty-five tons--the "Two Brothers"--to
carry their wares. The name of the vessel indicates that he is probably in
partnership with his brother, Nathaniel.

It is now important to take note of an activity which was to become a
consuming passion for the already overloaded businessman and planter. At this
time, Baltimore County created a type of militia known as rangers to protect
the citizenry from possible Indian reprisals. As the name suggests, they ranged
the countryside to protect any outlying settlers when there was trouble with
Indians. True, they were few because they had migrated westward. But
occasionally there were minor skirmishes and the people looked to the rangers
for their safety.

It was as a ranger that Christopher became knowledgeable about Indians
and the frontier of western Maryland and Pennsylvania. It was also his early
training ground for those later years on the trail. As it turned out, Christopher

> . . . combined his ranger work with fur trading. He gradually expanded his
> area of influence into western Pennsylvania, and even into the Ohio country.
> It was his work as a ranger that allowed Gist to become so well informed on
> Indian affairs that he could later be an effective agent for the Ohio
> Company.[12]

Enough has been said to explain Christopher's possible attraction to the
trail. He cleared roads, he could read a compass, he undoubtedly traded with
Indians who exchanged furs for the many supplies at the plantation store. He
must have trapped and hunted some on the fringe of woods that surrounded
his home.

Perhaps the hard times ahead will push Christopher away from the
settled life he had known. Between 1743 and 1745 Christopher and Nathaniel
became involved in a number of debts and were sued for recovery of these

---

[10]Ibid., p. 11.

[11]Ibid., p. 11.

[12]Kenneth P. Bailey, Christopher Gist, pps. 20-21.

obligations. One loss followed another until Christopher was forced to sell land inherited from his father as well as land he had purchased.[13] Next to go were slaves, furniture, tools, horses and his sloop.[14]

It seemed the losses would never end. In 1745, two more tracts of land, "Gist's Meadows" and "Elleges Folly," had to be sold. Later that year, two more lots were put up for sale. One was described as ". . . in Baltimore Town, lying on the water with a good Brick Dwelling House, well furnished, a Kitchen, Stable, Prize House and sundry other Outhouses with a good Garden paled in."[15] One blow after another in rapid succession was enough to shake the stoutest frame.

One of the original major contributing factors to Christopher's succession of losses was a fire which had devastating consequences.

> In 1732 he met a disaster which was to follow him the rest of his life. Like his father before him, his storehouses, filled with furs, was destroyed by fire. The British Fur Company pressed a claim for the amount of £10,000 sterling for the lost furs. Gist was broke. During the rest of his life, he paid on this claim, but never to the legal satisfaction of the agents of the fur company.[16]

Christopher finally left Baltimore Town and its environs with little of his fortune left. He must have made a stopover in Virginia on his way to his new home on the Yadkin River in North Carolina. While there, he sold "Gist's Limepits," a tract he had inherited from his father.[17] We will be hard pressed to know for sure whether the crushing losses pushed or the lure of the woods pulled him to the isolated settlement on the Yadkin. He was here and that was enough.

The rushing streams and well foliated trees must have been a soothing relief from the failures of Baltimore Town. The new life of farming, trapping, hunting and trading near the Great Warpath used in the intermittent warfare between the Iroquois and Cherokees was a welcome change for Christopher and his brood.

By 1750, at the age of forty-five, he had survived in the woods and learned enough about Indian trails to earn a reputation as a scout--at least enough of a reputation to be hired by the Ohio Company to explore a large

---

[13]Ibid., p. 12.

[14]Ibid., p. 12.

[15]Ibid., p. 12.

[16]Kenneth P. Bailey, Op. Cit., pps. 22-23.

[17]Christopher Johnston, Op. Cit., p. 376.

territory beyond the great chain of mountains. In doing this, Christopher Gist was to precede Daniel Boone by eighteen years--no mean accomplishment.

The Ohio Company, a Virginia-based group of gentlemen speculators, had persuaded the King in Council that it was in England's interest to populate the trans Appalachian region to ward off the encroachments of the French who also had claims to the territory. At the same time, there was money to be made by sub-dividing the land and selling it to land hungry settlers and from trading with the Indians. They were in need of a tough, reliable scout to find out exactly where their property was located and where the best land for settlement was situated. Christopher seemed to be just the man for the job and he was offered £150 for his labors.[18]

Christopher, in addition to the many skills he had acquired during his life, was a lucky find for the Company for other reasons. He was reported to be a gentleman in his demeanor, even though there was much coarseness or even crudeness among the various woodsmen. He was also physically imposing and capable of enduring much pain without complaint.

> There is no contemporary portrait of Christopher Gist, but it is known that he was taller than average, huskily built and of a dark complexion. If he was physically like Nathaniel, then he was about six feet, two inches tall, and weighed about two hundred pound.[19]

This made him appear like a giant to both Indian and fellow colonists -- especially when it is remembered that the average height of a soldier during the French and Indian War was about five feet, five inches tall.

Efforts to form the Ohio Company started in 1747 with an application for a grant of land from the Governor and Council of Virginia. When no immediate action was taken on their behalf, the committee of thirteen members wrote to an influential London merchant, John Hanbury, asking him to represent them in acquiring the grant in return for a share in the Company.

Hansbury's influence and energies were rewarded when in 1749 Lieutenant Governor Gooch received instructions from the King granting some 200,000 acres of land beyond the Allegheny mountains. Further, if certain conditions were met regarding the construction of a fort and the successful recruitment of settlers, the Company would be given an additional 300,000 acres. All seemed to be going well.

By 1749, the Company had the full twenty members provided for in its charter.[20] The names represent the elite of Virginia: George Fairfax, John Carlyle, George Mason, John Mercer, Lawrence Washington and the Governor

---

[18]Lois Mulkearn, George Mercer Papers, P. 5.

[19]Kenneth P. Bailey, Op. Cit., p. 15.

[20]Op. Cit., p. XI.

of Virginia, Robert Dinwiddie. It can readily be seen that all the members of the Company had at least two reasons for being alarmed at all the incoming reports of increased French activity to the north. First, they were Englishmen who had a dislike for the French as they were about to enter the fourth war since 1690 between these rival powers. Second, they were, after all, land speculators who stood to lose a great deal if the French should prevail.

The collision of forces in the making actually began at about the same time by both parties. The French had in mind the completion of a chain of forts forming a giant arc which would secure their water trade routes--the sweep of which would take in the St. Lawrence and Great Lakes in the north and the Ohio and Mississippi on the west. The Atlantic would be linked to the Gulf of Mexico and at the same time the British would be permanently contained on the Atlantic side of the Appalachians. Eventually it will be decided who will control North America. Small wonder that with so much at stake, both powers were secretly maneuvering for war while publicly declaring for peace.

French expansion accelerated in the year 1747 with the arrival in Canada of a new Governor, De La Galissoniere. He quickly commissioned an expedition under the leadership of Captain Celoron de Blainville to enter the Ohio region and reassert the right of France to rule the region. This was to be accomplished by burying lead plates at several strategic places to remind all comers that they were trespassers on French soil. The words inscribed upon these plates read as follows:

> Year 1749 in the reign of Louis XV, King of France, We, Celoron, Commanding the detachment sent by the Marquis de la Galissoniere, Commandant General of New France, to re-establish tranquility in certain Indian Villages in these cantons, have buried this plate at the meeting of the Ohio and Tchadokoin this 29th July, as a mark of the renewal of possession which we had formerly taken of the aforesaid river Ohio and all its feeders, and all territory upon both sides of the aforesaid streams as former Kings and France have enjoyed or ought to have enjoyed, and which they have maintained by force of arms and by treaties, especially by those of Ryswick, Utrecht, and Aix-la-Chapelle.[21]

On other occasions, the French claimed a right to control the area on the basis of the discoveries of the great French explorer, La Salle. These words do not seem to allow room for compromise.

To back up their threats with power, they started the construction of several forts which would give effective control of the Ohio country. Presque Isle, Le Bouef and Venango, all on or near the lower side of Lake Erie were the first to be built. This would be followed by a much larger fort at the "Forks" where the Allegheny merged with the Monongahela to form the Ohio.

Christopher Gist, as an agent for the Ohio Company, became involved in the tangle of rival claims which eventuated into the fourth of a series of wars

---

[21]A. G. Bradley, The Fight With France For North America, pps.43-4.

between England and France which has been called the French and Indian War (1756-1763.) Could Christopher possibly have forseen that in a mere four years he would be a part of that fateful event where shots would be fired that would plunge these two inveterate enemies into what has been called the "real" First World War?

As he crouched in the sweatbox during that awesomely frigid and blustery winter of 1750, could he possibly have imagined the many perilous days that lay ahead from unfriendly Indians, swollen streams, inhospitable terrain, and the usual bouts with dysentery, scurvy and smallpox? Was it now too late to back out? Christopher left no record which tells of such fears. As the fever dropped and strength returned, Christopher packed his goods into the tarp, tied it on the back of a horse and started down the slippery trail toward the "Forks" and on into the Ohio Country. The time for meditation had ended--now it was time for action.

Chapter II

Exploring the Ohio Country - 1750-51

On September 11, 1750, a committee of the Ohio Company drafted the instructions to be given to Christopher which outlined their expectations about his mission to explore the vast grant of land they had received from the Crown. In part, they read as follows:

> "You are to go out as soon as possible to the Westward of the great mountains, and carry with you such a number of Men as you think necessary, in Order to search out and discover the Lands upon the River Ohio & other adjoining Branches of the Mississippi down as low as the great Falls"[1]

Christopher was also expected by these instructions to show locations of mountains, passes through the mountains, and to describe the types of soil, take note of what Indian tribes lived in the various villages, get accurate locations of good, level land suitable for starting settlements and to make a map of his trip westward. Finally, he was to keep a Journal to give to the Company upon his return which would help the Company develop their land.

It was not until late October, 1750 that Christopher was ready for the trail. After getting his supplies together, he "set out from Colonel Thomas Cresap's at the old Town on Potomac River in Maryland along an old Indian Path . . . .[2] Christopher relied on well established warrior paths and trails used by traders because the woods were nearly impenetrable to the side of these well worn wilderness highways.

From the start, as he headed toward the Juniata River, Christopher had bouts of sickness. But his determination was steadfast. Resting for short periods seemed to bring some relief and days when the weather was so bad he could not travel helped dispel fevers and fatigue. Still, he had to eat and Christopher noted that he "killed a young Bear so that we had provision enough."

After nineteen days on the trail, while near "Loylhannan" (the present site of Ft. Liganier), Christopher became very sick and, as he noted in his Journal, sweated himself "according to the Indian Custom in a Sweat-House, which gave Me Ease, and my Fever abated"[3] To make a sweat-house a small, fairly air-tight enclosure was constructed out of leaves and limbs. Heated stones

---

[1]William M. Darlington, <u>Christopher Gist's Journals</u>, P. 31. Hereafter, this source will be referred to as "<u>Journals</u>" and means Journal I.

[2]William M. Darlington, <u>Journals</u>, P. 32.

[3]Ibid,. P. 33.

were then dropped into water to produce steam such as is in a steam bath. Feeling much better, Christopher was now ready to move on toward "The Forks" (now Pittsburgh) and on into the Ohio Country.

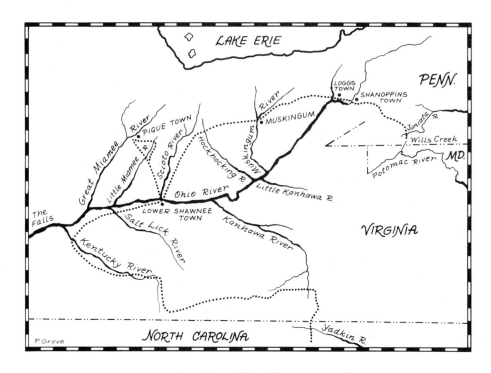

Approximate Route Taken By Gist 1750-51[4]

On the evening of the 19th of November, Christopher and his servant entered a small Delaware Indian town called Shannopins (now Pittsburgh, Pa.). Again, not feeling well they decided to rest here several days. He noted in his Journal that he took time to secretly set his compass because "it was dangerous to let a Compass be seen among these Indians." The Delawares were very suspicious of the intentions of the English and as the conflict progressed they became bitter enemies who had no limits on the cruelty and torture they would inflict on their enemies.

They saw in the Compass a sign of the intention of Europeans to settle upon their ancient hunting lands, and with it, the loss of their much needed game. Both the English and the French accused each other of wanting to take Indian lands and each tried to stir up the wrath of the Indians against their enemy. Both great powers repeatedly denied to the Indians any intention of

---

[4]The foregoing map to help the reader follow Gist is adapted from "A Portion of Lewis Evans's Map of 1755, with Pownall's 1776 Additions."

usurping Indian territories while assuming the right to occupy at will in the interest of empire.

These suspicions surfaced again at Loggs Town (now Economy, Pa.) further down the Ohio. The hostility was so evident that Christopher reported that he might not "go home safe again." But, he was able to remove their distrust by calling on the name of two of their heroes, George Croghan and Andrew Montour and by telling them that he had an important message from the King to deliver.

It was now late November and Christopher was ready to break away from the shores of the Ohio River and set out by trail toward Muskingum. He now had the company of several traders and noted that he had shot twelve turkeys - more than enough to feed all handsomely.

On September 5th, Christopher was at Elk's Eye Creek and pressing toward Margarets Creek. After several straight days on foot, Christopher entered the "Wyendott" settlement at Muskingum (now Coshocton, Oh.). Wyandots were also called "little Mingoes," a term given to Iroquois Indians who had moved westward from the established areas of the Six Nations.

On December 25th, Christmas Day, Christopher thought it would be a good thing to celebrate the day with some kind of religious ceremony using some readings of the Church of England. The message was interpreted by Andrew Montour and was received attentively by the Indian audience. They must have been favorably impressed because they adopted Christopher and gave him the name "Annosanah" - the name of a good man who had formerly lived among them. This service has been claimed to be "the first Protestant religious service ever held within the limits of the present State of Ohio."[5]

What followed the next day would seem to indicate that European religious rites did little to alter native customs. A woman prisoner was recaptured after a failed attempt to escape. As punishment, she was taken outside the village where she was surrounded by her captors who took turns at hitting her violently. "They then stuck her several Times, thru the Back with a Dart to the Heart, scalped Her, & threw the Scalp in the Air, and another cut off her Head."[6] Indian capacity for torture and mutilation has been a source of amazement to others. But humanly perpetrated suffering, if style is not a factor, was well distributed on all sides.

Christopher had been at Muskingum for some time. A new year had arrived and it was time to move on. The day before leaving the Wyandot camp (Jan. 14, 1751), he requested the presence of the Chief and Council to a meeting, the purpose of which was to invite the Indians to come to Virginia to receive gifts from the governor. But they declined because they were not empowered to act without the approval of other chiefs.

Moving westward, Christopher came to White Woman's Creek and on past the great swamp to the Delaware town of "Hockhokin." He noted in his Journal that the area had much fine, level land with scattered woods in which large walnut, hickory, poplar, cherry and sugar trees abounded. The trail now turned southward along the "Sciodoe" (Scioto) River, leading to a small

---

[5] Ibid., P. 113.

[6] Ibid., P. 39

Delaware town made up of about twenty families. There was an abundance of wild rye nearby so it made good sense to rest and feed the horses.

The next day Christopher attended a Council meeting with the Delawares. The speaker first made a presentation of four strings of wampum before warmly assuring the guests that his people were on the side of the English. The interpreter, Andrew Montour, gave the following report.

> "We the Delawares return you our hearty Thanks for the News You have Sent Us, and we assure You, We will not hear the Voice of any other Nation for We are to be directed by You our Brothers the English and by none else: We shall be glad to hear what our Brothers have to say to us at the Loggs Town in the Spring, and to assure You of our hearty Good will and Love to our Brothers We present You these four Strings of Wampum."[7]

While there was no assurance that these promises of friendship would stand, English interests in this region appeared optimistic in the upcoming struggle with France. For the present Christopher's hand at diplomacy was looking good. But it must be remembered that he was traveling with a trader of renown, George Croghan, who also carried much weight with the Indians. It was time to move on.

After a day of travel, Christopher and his companions arrived at "Shanoah Town" at the mouth of the Scioto River. It was a large encampment with about 300 men and occupied both sides of the river. The Shawnee leaders also professed to be friendly to the English and were invited to Loggstown in the Spring to receive gifts. Giving gifts was an expected and accepted practice in all dealings with Indians. Attempting to do business in the absence of presents was to invite failure. Their speaker gave an acceptance speech, part of which was interpreted as follows:

> "We shall be glad to hear what our Brothers will say to us at the Loggs Town in the Spring, and We hope that the Friendship now subsisting between Us and our Brothers, will last as long as the Sun shines or the Moon gives light-- We hope that our Children will hear and believe what our Brothers say to them, as We have always done, and to assure You of our hearty Good-Will towards You our Brothers, We present you with these four Strings of Wampum."[8]

The stay with the Shawnees must have been interesting and enjoyable because Christopher remained with them for almost two weeks while there he was an eye witness to a most unusual Indian custom. It must have made a deep impression because he described this "very extraordinary kind of Festival at which I was present and which I have exactly described at the end of my Journal."[9]

> "In the Evening a proper Officer made a public Proclamation that all the Indians marriages were dissolved, and a Public Feast was to be held for three

---

[7]Ibid., P. 43.

[8]Ibid., P. 45.

[9]Ibid., P. 46.

succeeding days after, in which the women as their Custom was were again to choose Husbands.

The next Morning early the Indians breakfasted and after spent the Day in dancing till the Evening when a plentiful Feast was prepared, after feasting they spent the night in dancing. The same Was the spent two Days till Evening, the Men dancing by themselves and then the Women in turns around the fires and dancing in their Manner in the Form of the Figure 8 about 60 or 70 at a time. The Women the whole Time they danced sang a Song in their Language the Chorus of which was, I am not afraid of my Husband I will choose what Man I please singing these Lines alternately. The third day in the evening, the men being about 100 in Number, same Times at Length, at other Times in a Figure 8 quite round the Fort and in and out of the long House, where they held their Councils, the Women standing together as the Men danced by them; and as any of the Women liked a Man passing by she stepped in and joined in the Dance, taking hold of the Man's Strand whom she chose, and then continued in the Dance till the rest of the Women stepped in and made their choice in the same manner: after which the Dance ended and the All retired to consummate."

It was now near the middle of February and Christopher did not cross the Ohio into what is now Kentucky at this time. Rather he took a nearly 200 mile swing to the Northwest toward the Big Miamis river to resist the Twigtwees, a tribe of the Miamis.

He was favorably impressed with the area, noting it to be... "fine, rich level Land, well watered with a great number of little Streams or Rivulets and full of beautiful natural Meadows, Covered with wild Rye, blue Grass and Clover, and abounds with turkeys, Deer, Elks and most Sorts of Game particularly Buffaloes, thirty or forty of which are frequently seen feeding in one meadow: In Short it wants Nothing but Cultivation to make it most delightful"[10]

When starting this northward leg of his journey, Christopher noted in his Journal that he had "left my Boy to take care of my horses in the Shannoah Town."[11] This has been wrongly interpreted as a reference to his son. The "Boy" referred to was the black, 17 year old servant already mentioned. He only took a son on one trip--the second one--which will be looked at later. At this point, George Croghan and Andrew Montour have temporarily joined him.

While a guest in the Twigtwee Town, now Piqua, Ohio, Christopher made great efforts toward strengthening their friendship by helping to repair an old Indian fort which was in need of new logs. But the Twigtwees apparently paid a terrible price for their pro-English stance. The record shows that, "This fort was attacked and captured by a force of about two hundred and forty Indians, led by two Frenchmen, June 22, 1752. The old King called Brittain, was taken, killed and eaten near the fort in the presence of his tribe."[12] Again, it should not be forgotten that the fiction of peace between England and France was maintained until 1756 although many acts of war were being perpetrated. But

---

[10]Ibid., P. 47

[11]Ibid., P. 46.

[12]Ibid., P. 125.

each side did not yet feel the opportune time was yet at hand for a formal declaration. A small digression is in order about the foregoing account of cannibalism, As Parkman wrote about another incident, "His heart is said to have been eaten by his murderers, to make them courageous; a practice not uncommon around Indians, after killing an enemy of acknowledged bravery."[13] Among the Indians, the belief persisted that by partaking of the victim's body they would be endowed with the qualities of the slain warrior.

Sometimes, however, ritual cannibalism merged gradually into simple cannibalism even if the distinction is merely academic to the uninitiated. On one occasion, Pontiac, an Ottawa warrior of known courage, was publicly upbraided by another chief for crossing this important line. He declared,

> "But as for you Pontiac, You have taken prisoners upon the lake and upon the river, and after having brought them to Your camp you have killed them and drunk their blood and eaten their flesh. You did it not in the manner of our - and your - custom, immediately after battle, when the flesh of the enemy is devoured so that you may take onto ourselves his strength and courage. No! You did it deliberately when the time for custom was past. Is the flesh of men good for food? No! One eats only the flesh of deer and other animals which the master of Life has placed on the earth for that purpose."[14]

Cannibalism was only one of the barbarian and cruel practices which are recorded during this period. Bodily mutilation and tortures of the most unspeakable types were inflicted upon captives by their Indian captors. Christopher could hardly have been unaware of these stories and surely realized what was in store for him if he should ever become the target of their wrath.

The month of February was now nearly gone and it was time to move back to the Lower Shawnee town and cross the Ohio. Before Christopher took leave, he participated in a most interesting ceremony on Sunday the 24th. Early that morning, four "French Indians" carrying a French flag came into the town. Their mission was to sway the Twigtwees over to the French. According to custom, they carried presents - in this case kegs of brandy, twists of tobacco and strings of wampum.

On Monday the Twigtwees made their formal reply. they began by responding most favorably to the English their speaker had this to say,

> "Brothers, We have heard what You have said to Us by the Interpreter and We see You take Pity upon our poor Wives and Children, and have taken US by the Hand into the great Chain of Friendship; therefore We present You with these two Bundles of Skins to make Shoes for your People, and this Pipe to smook in, to assure You that our Hearts are good and true towards You Our Brothers . . . .[15]

---

[13]Francis Parkman, The Conspiracy of Pontiac, Vol. I. Pps. 309-10.

[14]Allan W. Eckert, The Conquerors, P. 454.

[15]Ibid., P. 52.

As ambassadors for the British interests, Christopher and his party were again successful. They were ever mindful of the importance of winning the loyalty of as many tribes as possible prior to the outbreak of war.

On Tuesday, the Twigtwees gave their response to the French sympathizers. After rejecting French overtures, the speaker came out clearly for the English.

> ". . . We have made a Road as far as the Sea to the Sun-rising, and have been taken by the Hand by our Brothers the English . . . . and We assure You it is the Road We will go; and as You threaten Us with War in the Spring, We tell you if you are angry we are ready to receive you and resolve to die here before We will go to You, and that You may know that this our Mind, We send You this String of black Wampum.[16]

There could be no misunderstanding. All present knew that black wampum was a sign of war and white wampum a sign of peace. This was a final send-off for Christopher as he headed south to the banks of the Ohio.

Fearing that he might be surprised and harmed by the "French Indians" who were disappointed at the outcome of their mission, Christopher avoided the usual well marked trails and struck off through the underbrush. On the way he noted that, ". . . just at Night I killed a fine barren Cow - Buffaloe and took out her Tongue, and a little of the best of her Meat . . . ." He must have regarded tongue as a delicacy because this choice of food is reported several times. Luckily, all went well and he arrived at the Shannoah Town safely.

As he prepared to cross the Ohio and head southwest toward the Falls, (now Louisville, Kentucky) he was warned by a Mingo chief not to get too close because there were "French Indian" hunting parties nearby. They would most likely be in a hostile mood. But Christopher "resolved to venture as far as possible" since the Company desired his presence there. As it turned out, he came within twenty miles of the Falls.

As Christopher and his servant proceeded down the southeast bank of the Ohio he encountered two traders who gave him a large tooth - weighing over four pounds - which was supposed to be that of a mammoth or mastodon. Other bones had been found near the falls which included rib bones no less than eleven feet long and a skull bone claimed to be six feet across. Added to these were tusks upwards of five feet in length.[17]

On March 19, Christopher noted that he had crossed the "little Cuttaway River" - now known as the Kentucky River. This was his furthermost point from home. He would now be turning in a more easterly direction toward the Yadkin and home. It is not certain exactly which route he took at various points on his return. He could have made errors in his readings and some of the natural landmarks are not agreed upon.[18]

While on the Kentucky River, at a point where the Red River enters, Christopher gazed at land which was to be occupied eighteen years later by Daniel Boone. There are no records which reveal to what extent, if any,

---

[16]Ibid., P. 53.

[17]Ibid., Pps. 57-8

[18]See page 1248 especially. Charles A. Hanna, The Wilderness Trail, Vol. II.

Christopher had on Boone's decision to settle in Kentucky. But it is reasonable to believe that they shared stories as they traveled together later on Braddock's march - Boone as a wagoner and Christopher as a scout. They had a ready start as friends having already been neighbors on the Yadkin River.[19]

The weather was now moderating with an occasional warm day which made the trail more pleasant. He notes that he killed a buck elk and "took out his tongue to carry with us." But again he became so ill that he "sweated after the Indian Fashion" for a cure. This leg of the trip became extremely exhausting because they were forced to hack their way through dense laurel thickets.

March gave way to April. The days were much warmer, the snow had melted and there were signs of spring everywhere. This and the prospect of getting closer and closer to home enlivened the resolve of Christopher and his servant to outlast the weary trail. On the 15th, he reported that ". . .as I was climbing up the Rocks, I got a Fall which hurted me pretty much." But, hardened to pain, he kept to the trail and in the afternoon he had the good fortune to come across a bear which was devoured at the evening meal.

In early May, they crossed the "Big Conhaway" or New River on a raft of logs they had tied together. By the middle of the month they had crossed the dividing line between Virginia and North Carolina . On Saturday, the 18th, the trail-worn scouts were determined to reach home. But, there was a delay. As Christopher noted, ". . . When I came there I found all my Family gone, for the Indians had killed five people in the Winter near that place, which frightened my Wife and Family away to Roanoke about 35 M nearer in among the Inhabitants" . . . .[20]

The very next day, Christopher headed northward, arriving at the new home by nightfall and happily found his family well. He had been gone about seven months, experiencing extremes of weather and trail. He had mastered the rocky crags of the Appalachians and enjoyed the lush meadows north of the Ohio. He had gazed with awe at the blue grass in the Ken-to-ke region and outlasted the almost impassable stretches of laurel thicket toward the New River. It was good to be home.

But he was not yet cleared of all his duties. After some much needed rest he had to make a sketch of his route and write up a report to give to the gentlemen who made up the governing board of the Ohio Company.

After a brief visit with his family, Christopher made the long trip to Williamsburg, Virginia where he presented his Journal and a personal report. At this time, he recommended that a settlement be started in the area of the two Miami rivers. This was judged to be impractical because it was then much to far away from other settlements.[21]

The decision on the part of the Company to found settlements closer to Virginia's more established towns would require another trip westward to study

---

[19]See Kenneth P. Bailey, Christopher Gist, P. 45.

[20]Journal, P. 66.

[21]Lois Mulkearn, OP Cit., Pps. 49-50.

a different area.[22] So it came about that Christopher would face another winter trip to the trans Appalachian region but this time to the south of the Ohio between the Kanhawa and the Monongahela rivers. There was still some summer left as he departed Williamsburg for his new home in Roanoke which is to say still some time to enjoy his family before facing another endurance test in the wilderness. He reined his horse toward home.

---

[22]Ibid., P. 50.

Chapter III

Back to the Ohio Country - 1751-52

A committee of the Ohio Company met in Williamsburg on July 16, 1751 and drafted the instructions that Christopher was expected to follow on his second trip across the great mountains. They wanted him to

> ". . . look out & observe the nearest & most convenient Road You can find from the Company's Store at Will's Creek to a Landing at Mohanglyela (Monongahela).[1]

The importance of a road as an aid to the future development of the transmontane region cannot be overstated.   In the competition between Virginia and Pennsylvania for western trade, the Colony with a road was bound to win. The instructions continued. Christopher was asked to,

> ". . . proceed down the Ohio on the South Side thereof, as low as the Big Conhaway (Kanawha) and up the same as far as You judge proper and find good land. . . . "[2]

As on his first journey, he was also expected to make a map of the area, keep a journal which recorded his observations and invite the various Indian tribes to Logstown in the spring. He would again depart from the Company's store house at Wills Creek after getting horses and supplies.

It was early November before Christopher and his son[3] got underway through the gap in the mountains which opened the door to the west. With a steady pace they passed nearby what is now Frostburg and Castleman's along the general route later taken by General Braddock. By the 24th they were at "Turkey-foot" - near the present site of Confluence - not in the least deterred by wintry blasts in their faces.

Pressing further westward, they now came upon some land which took Christopher's eye. Even the barrenness of winter could not hide the awesome beauty of this rise of gentle rolling hills with a beautiful mountain as a backdrop. He marked this as a place for his family to settle some day as well as nearby sites for other settlers. "Gist's Plantation" was to become a landmark for travelers for many years. But, for now, he must keep to the trail. Nothing

---

[1]William M. Darlington, Christopher Gist's Journals, p. 67.

[2]Ibid., P. 67.

[3]The Journal does not name the son. Richard was now 22 years of age, Nathaniel 18 and Thomas 16.

unusual interrupted his passage through the naked forrests and the <u>Journal</u> notes only the routine killing of a turkey, bear or deer for food or gives special attention to a spread of well timbered land.

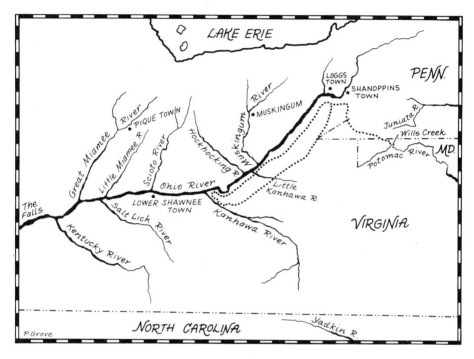

Approximate Route Taken by Christopher Gist
1751-52[4]

On December 7, with the winter days more threatening, the weary twosome entered an Indian camp not too far from the Monongahela River. Here, Christopher became acquainted with a Delaware Indian - Nemacolin - who was to make a name as a trail blazer. While in camp, Christopher extended an invitation to the Delawares to attend the Logstown conference in the spring. After another days rest, the two explorers moved on toward the crossing at the Monongahela.

Soon they were on the other side of the broad river at a point just beyond the junction of the Youghiogheny. They then set their course toward the south bank of the Ohio. It was now the middle of December and the weather had become severely cold with much snow and strong winds. The trail-wise father made the most of it but the younger one "had the misfortune to have his Feet frost-bitten, which kept us much longer here than we had

[4]Adapted from the John Mercer Map - 1752

intended...."[5] Winter in the highlands is relentless on all and deadly on those who misread her signs.

It was almost four weeks before the young scout could walk the rugged trail without pain. Then came even heavier snows which would not permit travel. December passed into January bringing the new year - 1752 - with it. The isolated barrenness of these snow-capped hills made them yearn for a warm fireside meal with the rest of the family back at Wills Creek. But, Christopher was not one to look backward. His mind was looking ahead to the next river to cross.

Their spirits were raised when on January the 22nd they were finally able to travel twelve miles. They slept that night in the cleft of a rock "where we Scared a Panther from under a Rock where there was Room enough for us...."[6] More bad weather prevented travel except at the slowest pace. Only iron- willed determination kept them on the trail.

On February 14, Christopher reported that they were now encamped along side a creek where they had come upon a large flat stone high on its bank. Taking out of his pack a large "cold chizzel," Christopher inscribed the following message in large letters."[7]

THE OHIO COMPANY
F E B^y 1751
BY CHRISTOPHER GIST

As the weary travelers trudged onward, there was undoubted elation when on February 18 they "coud see over the Conhaway River." Going downstream along the Big Kanawha, they came to the Ohio River (near Point Pleasant) and to the furthermost point of their trip. They would now start their return to Wills Creek.

After taking note of the land around the river, these trail-worn scouts turned northward closer to the south bank of the Ohio. On the 1st of March they were back to the Little Kanawha. With March came some moderation in the weather and much better progress on the trail. They discovered a large cave "much used by Buffaloes and Elks" which came there to lick the clay which had a salty taste.

They slept in the mammoth cavity that night and noted that not far from the entrance a herd of 30 elk were grazing. Christopher's son killed one of these large animals for much needed food. Then it was the trail again - still toward the north.

On the 7th of March they reported crossing "Wealin or Scalp Creek" (near Wheeling, W. Va.) where they camped for the night. The next day they moved still further northward to explore the land around Two Creeks. The land was most pleasing and had fine stretches of timber. It was now time to set a more direct course toward home. Heading eastward, they traveled until

---

[5] Ibid., P. 72.

[6] Ibid., P. 73.

[7] Ibid., P. 74. Interpreters are at a loss to explain why 1752 was not used.

they rejoined the old trail at the camp where the younger scout had experienced frost bite.

Then Christopher wrote the following entry into his Journal for the 12th of March. "I set out for Mohangaly (Monogahela) crossed it upon a Raft of Logs from whence I made the best of my Way to Potomack."[8] Using approximately the same route they had used on their way out, the two weary scouts ended their five month journey at the Company's Store House at Wills Creek on Sunday, March 29.

As they neared the end of the journey, Christopher took note of a rather interesting encounter with an Indian who asked a delicate question. He said that the great men of the Delaware nation "desired to know where the Indian's Land lay for that the French claimed all the Land on one side of the River Ohio and the English on the other Side. . . .?[9] Realizing that a wrong response would arouse extreme hostility, Christopher exhibited considerable diplomatic skill by his reply.

Said he, "My Friend, We are all one King's People and the different Colour of our Skins makes no Difference in the King's Subjects; You are his People as well as We if You will take Land & pay the King's Rights You will have the same Priveleges as the White People have and to hunt You have Liberty everywhere so that You don't kill the White People's Cattle & Hogs."[10] The response must have been acceptable to the Indians because they invited Christopher to "Come and live upon that River where (he) pleased."

After making his report to the Ohio Company, Christopher began plans to return to the beautiful tract of land he had picked for his family beyond the mountains near the Youghiogany.[11] But these plans had to be set aside for the moment because he had again become a representative for the Ohio Company. Governor Robert Dinwiddie had made arrangements for the conference at Logstown to begin in April and wanted him to attend. Also present were Colonel Joshwa Fry, Lunsford Lomax and Colonel James Patton. Acting as interpreters were Andrew Montour and Conrad Weiser. The presents for the Indians were carried to the meeting by Thomas Cresap. The celebrated trader. George Croghan was the commissioner from Pennsylvania.[12] The main purpose of the Logstown meeting was to "confirm the Lancaster Treaty of 1744 in which the Virginians claimed that the Indians had acknowledged the right of the Colony of Virginia to the lands upon the Ohio River."[13] In the instructions to Christopher from the Company they pointed to the expenses they had incurred so far in developing their land and that they were hard pressed to get the settlement process started in order to realize some profit for

---

[8]Ibid., P. 77.

[9]Ibid., P. 78.

[10]Ibid., P. 78.

[11]Gist's Plantation was located just north of Uniontown, Pa. on highway 119.

[12]Lawrence A. Orrill, Christopher Gist and His Sons, p. 199.

[13]Ibid., P. 199.

their efforts. But, at the same time, they must avoid any chance of friction with their Indian neighbors.

The Company had a right to such expectations because, as they expressed it, "they have an indisputable right to do" so "as our bretheren the six nations sold all the land to the westward of Virginia at the Treaty of Lancaster."[14] Would the Western Indians accept their interpretation of the treaty and then honor their claim? Hopefully, the conference would remove all doubt.

On June 1st, 1752, the long awaited Logstown conference got underway. It lasted just two weeks. After much ceremony and heated speeches, and with the invaluable assistance of Andrew Montour, the parties came to an agreement which would allow the Virginians to proceed. Christopher's signature appeared on the treaty.

One can judge the importance of these proceedings to some extent by the exchanges of presents and the number of strings of wampum which changed hands. Aside from a brass kettle, tobacco and cloths, there were no less than twenty-five presentations of one or more strings of wampum to the parties attending.[15]

Two Delaware leaders - Shingiss and the Beaver - welcomed Christopher and the other representative to the town. They were dressed in their finest apparel - even silver breast plates adorned their bodies.

Giving two strings of wampum, one of the chiefs began the conference with this oration:

> "Bretheren of Virginia and Pennsylvania, I desire you will hearken to what I am going to say that you may open your hearts and speak freely to us. We don't doubt but you have many things in your minds which may trouble you notwithstanding which we hope we may continue in friendship on which we give you these strings of Wampum."[16]

With such a flourish as a start and with intermittent exchanges of wampum, the conference progressed with much good will.

Then George Croghan, representing the governor of Pennsylvania, helped the cause by speaking on behalf of the representatives of Governor Dinwiddie. After presenting a string of wampum, he made a direct appeal "to the Indians letting them know that it was his desire that they should receive their bretheren of Virginia kindly . . . ."[17] Croghan's word carried great weight with his Indian listeners.

The appeal made, the Virginians now waited anxiously for the reply. The Half-King (Tanacharison) was the first Indian to speak - saying that it was their desire that a stronghouse (fort) be built at the fork of the Monongahela. He then asked the commissioners to send only decent traders among the Indians because they did not want to deal with those who were unscrupulous

---

[14]Lois Mulbearn, Op. Cit., P. 53.

[15]For a complete record of the speeches made see Ibid., pps. 54-66.

[16]Ibid., p. 55.

[17]Ibid., p. 55

in overcharging for their goods. They also brought too much spirituous liquors with them.

There were other concerns which were addressed including the report that John Frazer, a well respected gunsmith, had planned to vacate the area. If true, another was needed immediately because the Indians were not skilled at gun repair. Several other misunderstandings were cleared up before the meetings ended.

Christopher apparently only spoke once. At this time he presented a string of wampum and a suit of Indian clothing for the commissioners from Virginia to the Six Nations "to wipe away their tears for the loss of one of their chiefs who lately came down from the head of Ohio to Logstown and died there."[18] This kind of ceremonial expression of good will made it possible for Christopher to be successful continually in negotiations with the Indians.

The Ohio Company was now in a better position to lay out their lands for settlement. But, events elsewhere were moving quickly to produce a confrontation which would end the Company's chances for success. When the French, under the leadership of Captain Contrecouer, overwhelmed the small detachment of Virginians at "The Forks" in the spring of 1754, they preempted any further migration into the Ohio region.

With the outbreak of war in 1756, they would be stalled completely during seven long years of fighting between France and England. The final blow to their hopes came with the Proclamation of 1763 which forbade any migration across the great mountains. The Company would never recover from this devastating series of blows. They were the unfortunate victim of events over which they had no control.

But we must now return to Christopher and his efforts to build a settlement in the Ohio country. With the Logstown conference behind him, he could now think about a homestead on the beautiful tract of land which he had found so desirable on his second journey. But, again there were delays.

He had assured the Company after a trip through Maryland and Pennsylvania that about fifty families had agreed to move near his settlement as soon as they could be given adequate supplies.[19] Meeting the demands of recruiting kept Christopher from devoting the time needed for his own family.

Then there was need to clear a road over which the settlers could haul their families and supplies. In April, 1752, Christopher got his instructions from the Company to open up such a road. They were as follows:

> "If Colo. Cresap has not agreed with any person to clear a Road for the Company, You are with the advice and assistance of the said Colo. Cresap to agree with the proper Indians who are best acquainted with the ways Immediately to cut a Road from Will Creek to the Fork of Mohongaly at the cheapest rate you can for Goods and this you may mention publickly to the Indians at the Loggs Town or not as you can see Occasion."[20]

---

[18]Ibid., p. 61.

[19]Lois Mulkearn, Op. Cit., pps. 238-9.

[20]Ibid., p. 147.

How much work was done on the road is not certain. But some planning and clearing did occur because Christopher was paid over 44 by the Company for work and expenses. The path was widened enough for pack horses and later was extended to a width of twelve feet by General Braddock's workmen. This wilderness trail would eventually become a highway.

Much has been made of the assistance given by the Delaware scout - Nemacolin. His name has been linked to those of Gist and Cresap in the folklore of the frontier. It has been suggested that some exaggeration has taken place about the extent of his help in building this road. A look at the records of the Ohio Company shows seven entries relating to clearing this road but that he is not mentioned as being employed. Christopher takes note of Nemocolin only once in his second Journal.[21] In all probability his help, whatever the extent, was most welcome.

Not until the fall of 1752 did Christopher and his family settle on the "Gist Plantation."

Gist Plantation Sign On Highway 119 North of Uniontown

In doing so, he "established the first farm home west of the Allegheny Mountains."[22] There is no agreement about how many families settled

---

[21] Ibid., pps. 555-6.

[22] Jean Muir Dorsey and Maxwell J. Dorsey, Op. Cit., p. 16.

nearby but the best estimate for the early period seems to be eleven.[23] The difficulty comes about because of families coming and leaving. Recruitment brought in new families but fear of Indians accounted for the losses. A letter of that time reported that,

> ". . . some of their People are returned being seized with a Panic on the Threats of the French and their seizing all they can lay their hands on belonging to the British Subjects and its further surmized that they spirit up the Indians in their interest, to way lay them and murder them."[24]

This fear of the French and their Indian allies must have been a powerful deterrent to settlers when it is remembered what an attractive offer the Ohio Company made to them. Each family would receive 100 acres for each of the first four members and 50 acres for each additional person. After living on the land for three years, they were expected to pay four pounds sterling for every one hundred acres. In addition, the land would be free of quit rents for the first five years.[25] With such inducements, an industrious family could achieve independence and a good living on one of these tracts of land opened up by the Company.

As the skirmishes between the two belligerent powers increased, the settlement was not able to survive. On July 5, 1754, after defeating Washington at Fort Necessity, De Villiers, the French commander destroyed everything belonging to Christopher and the other settlers. Homes, barns, fences and other outbuildings were burned as the French troops returned to Fort Duquesne.

This must have been an agonizing blow to Christopher. At 49 years of age the quest for property was as illusive as it was throughout a good bit of his adult life. He was completely without home or property again. His family had been uprooted several times in their search for a permanent homestead and it seemed that bad luck was to forever haunt the Gists.

Twice Christopher tried to petition the Virginia House of Burgesses for some compensation for his devastating losses. He was rejected both times. The published plea stated that,

> "Gist had settled there with his family and Colonel Washington with his troops had encamped on his Plantation and his horses and carriage being used in His Majesty's service, he could not remove his effects, worth about 200 pounds; they were taken by the French who set fire to his fences and all his horses. The fences had been used for palisades for Washington's troops. He was ready to risk his life and small fortune but wished to be compensated for his loses."[26]

[23] David Trimble, Op. Cit., p. 19.

[24] Ibid. p. 24.

[25] Lois Mulkern, Op. Cit., pps. 172-3.

[26] Helen Vogt, Westward of Ye Laurall Hills, p. 125.

Nor was the propensity to lose property and goods confined to Christopher. Bad luck seemed to bedevil his children. As one historian of the area has noted,

"There is a final ironic and rather sad twist to the affairs of the Gists in Penn's Southwest in certain Fayette County land transfers after the death in 1787 of Christopher's son, Thomas Gist. In order to pay a debt of nine pounds owed by Thomas, the Westmoreland sheriff seized the 400 acres where he had lived and sold it at public auction November 20, 1788, to the highest bidder, and Isaac Meason for a bid of thirty pounds began his acquisition of Gist land on which he founded his iron empire. In the spring of 1789 the Fayette County sheriff recovered against Anne Gist for 120 pounds by selling another Gist tract of 620 acres to Meason for thirty-one pounds. Five years later the Gists sued Meason and were able to make him pay a total of 1,200 pounds for 1,000 acres."[27]

Getting back to Christopher's fate, it is sad to report that he had to start all over again. Returning to Wills Creek and then to Winchester he became an invaluable source of help to Washington. Much more can be told about this period of Christopher's life later, but for now, to keep in sequence, we must pick up on the events which brought him into a friendship which was to last until he died. The young major who knocked at his door to request his help was none other than George Washington. He wanted Christopher to be his guide as they travelled toward Lake Erie to deliver a warning to the French that they were unwelcome in that region.

---

[27]Ibid., pps. 1125-6.

Chapter IV

Christopher Meets Major Washington

The summer of 1753 was a period of frantic activity and frustration for Christopher. The work of laying out and clearing the road from Wills Creek to "the Forks" had to be completed while at the same time the Ohio Company began pressing him for the construction of a fort nearby.

A committee of the Company passed a resolution on July 25 for immediate construction of this fort which was originally planned to be built at Shertees Creek, not too far from "The Forks."[1] As it turned out, the site of the fort was moved because of the recommendations of George Washington.

One source of satisfaction came that same month when Christopher got the long awaited word that he had finally been granted his surveyor's commission from William and Mary College.[2] The Company now wanted him to take readings on the road he was building as well as to lay out a town near their fort. There was much work to be done on the frontier but he was up to the demands.

All of this was interrupted by a request from the governor of Virginia to attend another Indian conference - this time at Winchester. The time was set for September. The object of the conference was to build on the results of the Logstown conference of the last year. There was need for more talks (and, of course, presents) to maintain the good will of the Indians in the Ohio region. Therefore, an invitation was given to the chiefs and sachems of the Six Nations to meet with a commission from Virginia headed by Colonel William Fairfax.

Andrew Montour was the interpreter while Christopher helped arrange the setting to make it conducive to negotiations between the Indians and their European hosts. This included - incredible as it may seem - being a godfather at the baptism of Monakatoocha's son, who now had the new name of "Dinwiddie."[3] Other dignitaries included George Fairfax, Lord Fairfax, Colonel James Wood and Captain William Trent.

Notable Indians present were Delaware George, Turtle, Raccoon and Big Kettle, to mention a few. After a week-long session and the appropriate number of exchanges of wampum and presents, there was agreement on several issues which had rankled relationships in the past. The French threat, too

---

[1]Lois Mulkearn, George Mercer Papers, p. 147.

[2]Ibid., p. 149.

[3]Stuart E. Brown, Jr., Virginia Baron: The Story of Thomas 6th Lord Fairfax, p. 127.

much spirituous liquors, invasion of Indian hunting grounds and the release of
several Shawnee prisoners were brought up and resolved for the moment.

On the most important question - Virginia's access to land in the Ohio
region - there was definite stalling.   The reluctant endorsement of the
Logstown agreement was not forthcoming. Future conferences could alter this
state of affairs but meanwhile the Ohio Company was anxious to move ahead
with their plans. Christopher returned to Wills Creek to await further orders.

This was not long in coming. In his third Journal, Christopher enters
this terse statement.

> "Wednesday 14 November, 1753. Then Major Washington Came to my house
> at Wills Creek and delivered me a letter from the Council in Virginia
> requesting me to attend him up to the Commandant of the French Fort on the
> Ohio River."[4]

The fort referred to was on a branch of the Alleghany which was regarded at
that time as the Ohio River. Washington had set out for Wills Creek from
Williamsburg on October 31. On the way he picked up some supplies and had
hired Jacob Vanbraam to be his interpreter.   After his meeting with
Christopher, he hired four other men as servants.

Christopher and the young Washington made a good team. He was now
forty-eight years of age and brought to the relationship a wealth of practical
knowledge about life in the woods and about how to deal with Indians.
Washington was only twenty-one but he was able as well as ambitious. They
must have immediately liked each other because they worked together with
much mutual respect until the senior scout died. The bewhiskered, buckskin-
clad woodman took the younger man under his wing and, as it turned out, this
was a stroke of good fortune for Washington.

The party - which now had grown to seven - were on their way almost
immediately to deliver a most important communication to the commandant
of the French forces on the Ohio from the governor of Virginia - Robert
Dinwiddie.

The letter, carried by Washington, first made several complaints of acts
of hostility to ward Englishmen by the French. It also charged them with
encroachmentsinto territory clearly known to belong to Virginia.
Then came the demand that could trigger into motion those actions and
reactions which lead to war. It read,

> "However Sir, in Obedience to my Instructions, it becomes my duty to require
> your peaceable Departure; and that you would forbear prosecuting a Purpose
> so interruptive of the Harmony and good Understanding which his Majesty is
> desirous to continue and cultivate with the most Christian King"[5]
>
> Christopher and his companions only traveled eight miles before they
> were overtaken by a messenger who informed him that his son "lay sick at the
> mouth of the Conegocheague."[6] He sought the judgement of the others who,

---

[4]William M. Darlington, <u>Christopher Gist's</u> <u>Journals</u>, p. 80 (Hereafter referred to as <u>Journals</u> and means #3)

[5]<u>Ibid</u>., p. 26.

[6]William M. Darlington, <u>Op</u>. <u>Cit</u>., p. 80 (Conococheague was the present site of Williamsport, Maryland)

after some debate, asked him to remain as a guide. With great reluctance and anxiety he wrote a letter and sent medicine to the ailing young man. This responsibility met, they were again on their way.

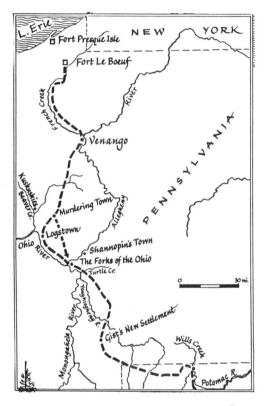

The Gist and Washington Journey 1753-54[7]

The path taken was the one Christopher had used on his second journey westward. This made it possible to stop for a short time at his home at the new settlement. Moving on, they came to the mouth of Turtle Creek where they shared the hospitality of the celebrated trader and gunsmith, John Frazier. On November 23, the trail-worn party reached "The Forks."

Washington was very impressed with this site and took some time to inspect the area. He then wrote in his journal a sentence which was to alter the original site of the proposed fort planned by the Ohio Company. He wrote,

"As I got down before the Canoe, I spent some time in viewing the Rivers, and the Land in the Fork, which I think extremely well situated for a Fort, as it has the absolute Command of both Rivers.[8]

---

[7]Adapted from the Journal of Major George Washington, pps. VI and VII. (Hereafter referred to as Journal.)

[8]George Washington, Op. Cit., p. 4.

Hence it was that the confluence of the Monongahela and Alleghany became the strategic location for a fort either by the British or the French.

While at "The Forks" they met with Shingiss, King of the Delawares, who agreed to travel to Logstown and meet with the Half-King and together they would plan how to deal with the French. They came to the agreement that the Half-King and a few hunters would travel along with the Virginians because he also had some words to say to the new commander.

The talks with the Half-King gave Washington an uneasy feeling. It started when this crafty chief began to probe about his business with the French. He could not say that he was warning the French to vacate land belonging to Virginia since the Indians present would be affronted at such a claim. They firmly believed the land belonged to Indians. He could, however, continue the old practice of warning the Indians about how devious and greedy the French were and how caring were the English. This strategy worked.

Actually, it soon came out that the Half-King had his own stories about the French that could match or even top those Washington could tell. The Half-King told of a meeting he had earlier with the former commander at Fort Le Boeuf. Pierre Paul, Sieur de Marin had the unmitigated gall to publicly ridicule this respected chief for telling the French officer that his soldiers and forts were not welcome in their land because ". . . the Great Being above allowed it to be a Place of Residence for us."

Perhaps the haughty French soldier could be forgiven for his arrogance. He was not only old and crotchety but near death - brought about by that ubiquitous scourge of the frontier - dysentery. His intemperate blast is hardly matched for its tactlessness. Said he,

> "Indian, I am troubled enough in this place with mosquitoes and flies. I do not need another pest here. Look around you. Yesterday the Miamis were fast friends of the English, but we ate their chief and today they bring us English scalps and ask for forgiveness. The Delawares and Shawnees come here and ask to carry our baggage for us, and all the other tribes of the Western lands rain on us their devotion. Yet you come here and dare to stand in our way and say that you present the Six Nations? You lie! You are a little man with big ideas. Go away from here before I flick you away as the horse flicks the fly with his tail. If you stay, I may have to spank you to teach you some respect."[9]

Nor was this all. The Half-King was told that the French would use whatever rivers they desired; build whatever forts they had in mind and would crush with sheer force any opposition. Washington could also read from this what answer he could expect to his letter. But he must get it formally from French authorities.

After several days on the trail the Virginians and their Indian allies were at Venango (now Franklin, Pennsylvania) where they were met in a kindly and polite way by Captain Philippe Thomas Joncaire who was in command. He advised Washington that he must go further north to Fort Le Boeuf and deal with an officer of higher rank. While Washington negotiated, Christopher busied himself with the Indian hunters and guides to work out the route they would take northward.

---

[9]Allan W. Eckert, Wilderness Empire, p. 242.

The short stay at Venango proved to be interesting but there were moments of anxiety. The French were constantly using intrigue to sway the Indians to desert their English companions. Rum and presents were readily supplied, keeping Christopher and Washington on alert with a watchful eye.

Washington gave this interesting account of what happened one evening at dinner.

> "The Wine, as they dosed themselves plentifully with it, soon banished the Restraint which at first appear'd in their conversations, and gave a License to their tongues to reveal their Sentiments more freely.
>
> They told me that it was their absolute Design to take Possession of the Ohio, and by G-- they would do it; for that they were sensible the English could raise two men for their one; yet they knew their Motions were too slow and dilatory to prevent any Undertaking of theirs"[10]

There could be little doubt that these intoxicated officers were reflecting the official attitude of French policy makers. Christopher and Washington took advantage of every opportunity to find out what they could about the fort, the number of troops and what intentions they had for the coming spring.

In spite of all of Washington's efforts to be on the move, they were detained by bad weather. Captain Joncaire used this opportunity to call a meeting with the Half-King to draw him to the French interest. Christopher noted that Joncaire ". . . did everything he could to prevail on our Indians to stay behind us, and I took care to have them along with us."[11]

Washington was markedly irritated at the bald attempt to win over the Half-King. He noted that Captain Joncaire, "made several trifling Presents and applied Liquor so fast, that they were soon render'd incapable of the Business they Came about. . . ."[12] But all their efforts to divide and conquer were to no avail and the Virginians got underway with their party intact.

Swollen streams and bad weather failed to stop the messengers from making it safely to Fort Le Boeuf (the site of present day Waterford, Pennsylvania). They were soon admitted to the cabin of the ranking French officer, Legardeur de St. Piere, who had only arrived at the fort seven days ahead of the Virginians.

It was now the middle of December. A speedy answer would allow a return trip before the onslaught of winter storms. While their message was being translated and studied, Christopher and Washington made a quick study of guns, troops and supplies. They estimated the number of birch-bark canoes to be about 50. There were also about 170 pine canoes and many more almost completed. They were, no doubt, almost ready for a spring offensive.

Again, at this fort, every ruse was tried to entice the Indians to desert the English cause. For three days the French used rum and presents without success. An exasperated Washington sent his helpers with their horses

---

[10] George Washington, Journal, p. 13.

[11] William M. Darlington, Journals, p. 82

[12] George Washington, Journal, p. 15.

southward toward Venango to signal a definite intention of leaving. Every day's delay was a risk of being held up indefinitely by snow storms.

On the evening of the 14th, Washington was given the answer he had been waiting for. Its contents came as no surprise in view of all the preliminary signs. Everything pointed to one fact; the French were there and they had no intention of leaving. As one officer had remarked in casual conversation,

> "The Country belonged to them, that no Englishman had a Right to trade upon those Waters; and that he had orders to make every Person Prisoner that attempted it on the Ohio or on the Waters of it."[13]

The new commander at Fort Le Boeuf did not mince words. After pleading ignorance about any claimed acts of hostility against the English, he wrote,

> "As to the Summons you send me to retire, I do not think myself obliged to obey it; Whatever may be your instructions, I am here by Virtue of the Orders of my General; and I entreat you, Sir, not to doubt one moment, but that I am determin'd to conform myself to them with all the Exactness and Resolution which can be expected from the best Officer.[14]

The letter was signed with the usual flourish of the day with "the profound Respect with which I am, Sir, Your most humble, and obedient Servant." This inflated capacity for diplomatic politeness did not obscure the reality that if push came to shove, force would be readily forthcoming to support French claims.

The return home would prove to be must trying from the start. Almost immediately they were hampered by snow and ice. As Christopher reported it, "The ice was so hard we could not break our way through, but were obliged to haul our vessels across a point of land and put them in the creek again."[15] At other times, the creeks were so low that they had to get out of their canoes and walk beside them in the water to keep from overturning while the water froze to their clothing. There was at least one moment of pleasure when a French canoe overturned sending kegs of wine and brandy floating downstream.[16]

The slow pace, frozen streams and sickly horses started to work on Washington's patience. He began to press Christopher to break away from streams and to set out on foot. But, wrote the seasoned scout " . . .

> I was unwilling he should undertake such a travel, who had never been used to walking before this time. But as he insisted on it, I set out with our packs, like Indians, and travelled eighteen miles. That night we lodged at an Indian

---

[13]Ibid., p. 18.

[14]Ibid., p. 27.

[15]William M. Darlington, Op. Cit., p. 84.

[16]Ibid., p. 84.

Cabin, and the Major was much fatigued. It was very cold; all the small runs
were frozen, so that we could hardly get water to drink.[17]

The inclination to be headstrong against the experience of others seemed
to be a trait of the younger scout in his earlier years. Over against this was a
strong sense of duty and perseverance which the grizzled, older scout must
have admired.

As they moved steadily southward, they met an Indian who agreed to
guide them by a shorter route to "The Forks." At this point they were pleased
at the prospect of a shorter route and were not suspicious of the Indian's
offering. But, as Christopher reported it, it was not long before there was cause
for suspicion.

". . . . the Indian took the Major's pack. We travelled very brisk for eight or ten
miles, when the Major's feet grew very sore, and he very weary."[18]

Taking note of Washington's condition, the Indian guide offered to carry the
Major's gun. This Washington refused to do since he was by now suspicious of
the over solicitous volunteer.

The situation suddenly became dangerous as the Indian inched forward
about fifteen paces - then suddenly turned and fired toward them. Fortunately
for both and for history, the bullet missed the mark and landed harmlessly in
a tree. The now frightened Indian ran ahead and quickly tried to reload his
gun. Before he could get the gun ready for firing, both scouts pulled him to the
ground. According to Christopher, he "would have killed him; but the major
would not suffer me to kill him."[19]   Christopher obeyed the orders even
though it was not to his liking. They now felt they must be on the trail all
night to put a safe distance between themselves and their would-be assailant.

Two days later, on the 29th of December, as they reached Shannopin's
Town on the Alleghany (now within the corporate limits of Pittsburgh,
Pennsylvania), they encountered another near tragedy. Washington recorded
this account of what happened.

"There was no Way for getting over (the Alleghany) but on a Raft, which we
set about, with but one poor Hatchet, and got finished just after Sun-setting,
after a whole Days Work; we got it launched, and on Board of it, and set off;
but before we were Half Way over, we were jammed in the Ice in such a
manner that we expected every moment our Raft to sink, and ourselves to
perish; I put out my setting Pole to try to stop the Raft, that the Ice might pass
by, when the Rapidity of the Stream threw it with so much Violence against
the Pole, that it jirked me out into ten Feet Water, but I fortunately saved
myself by catching hold of one of the Raft Logs. . . .[20]

---

[17]Ibid., p. 84.

[18]Ibid., p. 85.

[19]Ibid., p. 85.

[20]George Washington Journal, pps. 21-22.

The weary, waterlogged scouts were forced to camp that night on a small island in the middle of the Alleghany River. That they survived was probably due to the trail knowledge of the elder guide. In spite of the fact that his fingers were frost-bitten and that it was uncommonly cold, Christopher maintained his usual optimism. He wrote, "but the cold did us some service, for in the morning it was frozen hard enough for us to pass over on the ice."[21]

They then walked ten miles to John Frazier's cabin at the mouth of Turtle Creek where they were the recipients of much needed hospitality by the bearded gunsmith. His cabin was a landmark for traders, trappers and foot-weary Indians passing by.

Neither of these veterans of the woods embellished the two incidents in any of their writing. Christopher used the same matter of fact style in recording them as he did about shooting a buffalo or an elk. He was not given to exaggeration. Was he merely over modest? A few more details in either journal would tell us more about what really happened.

One of Christopher's biographers makes reference to this northern trip as "the celebrated journey in which Gist twice saved Washington's life."[22] This may well go beyond the facts since both participants were so scanty in their accounts of those two days on the trail. But if the claim is close to the mark, this nation is indeed in debt to the man who saved the leader of the American Revolution and the future first president of the New Republic. This alone would make him unrivaled among frontier scouts.

Washington and Christopher left the comforts of Frazier's cabin on January 1, 1754 and headed eastward toward the Gist estate at the new settlement. They remained there only one day and then only because of a driving, freezing rain that put a halt to all travel. After two more days on the trail they arrived at Wills Creek. While this was the end of the journey for Christopher, the major had to reach Williamsburg and deliver the letter to the governor.

On January the 11th, Washington rode up to Belvoir where he stopped a day for some much needed rest. On the 16th he presented the governor with his account of what had happened on this momentous journey. Dinwiddie had the journal published, making the young major a celebrity.

Events were now moving rapidly toward a series of confrontations which could only eventuate in armed conflict on a grand scale. Even before Christopher and Washington arrived at Wills Creek on the 6th of January, they met a convoy of no less than 17 horses loaded with material and tools needed to build a fort and supplies and stores to support troops. The governor of Virginia had taken the lead in meeting the French threat because he was well aware of their spring plans.

On February 17, 1754, Captain William Trent arrived at "The Forks" with orders to start construction. Christopher was already there and together they selected the site and began the work of clearing the underbrush and trees. Next to arrive was Ensign Edward Ward who also brought some workmen from

---

[21]William M. Darlington, Op. Cit., p. 86.

[22]Allen Johnson and Dumas Malone (Eds.), Dictionary of American Biography, p. 234.

Redstone Creek. Time was crucial - the French were undoubtedly aware of their presence.

The whole enterprise turned out to be a wasted effort. On April 17, the French made their appearance with an estimated 500 troops under the command of Captain Pierre de Contrecoeur who demanded an immediate surrender. The small band of Virginians had no choice but to capitulate and vacate the contended site. The defeated builders passed by Gist's new settlement on their way to Wills Creek. Meanwhile the triumphant French army destroyed the work there and started immediately to build a fort of their own. It was now called Fort Duquesne in honor of the Governor General of Canada, the Marquis Duquesne de Meneval.

Governor Dinwiddie was active on several fronts in his actions to repel the French intruders. He awarded Washington the new rank of Lieutenant Colonel and gave him command of 50 militia with the power to raise more.

When he arrived at Wills Creek on May 6, Washington got word of Ensign Ward's surrender. He determined to move westward to the Great Meadows and wait for more support before attacking the French forces. His men could also work on clearing more of the road.

The governor also wrote letters to the southern Indians - Catawbas, Cherokees and Chickasaws - asking for warriors in the cause against the French.

> "Brothers, I hereby invite you, in fact, urge you to now blow away the clouds before Your eyes and take up the hatchet against the French who, under pretense of embracing you mean to squeeze you to death[23]

For several reasons the response of the southern Indians was not very great. Nor were matters improved when appeals went out to neighboring colonies for support. Most could not believe the French were an imminent threat to their safety. In Pennsylvania, the Quakers, who were pacifists, would not vote to advance money on principle. Since they controlled the legislature - no action was taken. The final result was an unprotected frontier which left many outlying settlers to the mercy of the French and their savage allies.

The energetic governor fared a little better when the Virginia legislature voted ten thousand pounds for the defense of that colony. The governor had hoped for much more. Enraged, he wrote to his friend and Ohio Company partner, John Hanbury.

> "I am sorry to find them too much in a Republican way of thinking. I have had a great deal of trouble from the factious disputes and violent heats of a most imprudent, troublesome party here in regard to that silly fee of a pistole. Surely every thinking man will make a distinction between a fee and a tax. Poor people, I pity their ignorance and narrow, ill-natured spirits. . . ."[24]

This almost universal tardiness in keeping up with the demands of the moment would only lengthen the time required to expel the French from North America. This was the case again on May 26 when a detachment of 50 French

[23] Allan Eckert, Wilderness Empire, p. 261.

[24] Ibid., p. 262.

soldiers under the command of Ensign La Force appeared at Christopher's new settlement homestead and would have destroyed everything but for the intervention of some friendly Indians.

When he became aware of their presence, Christopher kept an eye on their movements and reported this intelligence to Colonel Washington who immediately dispatched him to Williamsburg to inform Governor Dinwiddie of the situation on the frontier.

While Christopher was on this mission, Washington had his first military engagement with the French. Upon receiving word from the Half-King about the presence of a small detachment of troops secluded behind an embankment of rocks just beyond the meadows, Washington determined that now was the time to strike.

After daylight, on May 28, Washington and his troops successfully ambushed a company of just over 30 French soldiers under the command of Ensign Coulon de Jumonville de Villiers. After a 15 minute skirmish, the battle was over with 10 Frenchmen dead, ten captured and one escaped. The young French officer, Jumonville, was among those killed. The rocky ravine just off the trail toward Fort Duquesne has been immortalized as the Jumonville Glen.

The prominent British statesman, Horace Walpole, later wrote about this encounter as, "the volley fired by a young Virginian in the backwoods of America that set the world on fire." A present statement would in all probability be more moderate since this was only a "precipitating cause." After all, this Anglo-French rivalry was to involve these great powers in no less than six confrontations between 1690 and 1814. Indeed, there were deeper causes than a minor engagement in the backwoods of North America.

Again, the Walpole claim needs even more examination when it is remembered that Washington will, within another two months, have a major defeat on his hands but that war was not declared for another two years. But Walpole is not aside the mark when he almost calls this war a "world war." Some students of the period have in fact called this war the "real" World War I.

In the aftermath of this pre-war skirmish - and for only a short period of time - the Gist plantation became a beehive of activity as a supply center for Washington's troops. Moreover, Christopher furnished horses and other supplies sometimes at his own expense.[25] After some deliberation, it was decided that this site was not a viable location to make a stand against the French and that it would be wiser to fall back to the Great Meadows and improve the fortification there. This make-shift defense was appropriately named Fort Necessity.

Christopher, in the meantime, had returned to The Meadows in June after trying to secure much needed supplies for any movement against the French. He was able to obtain some uniforms, powder and lead.[26] He was there in time to participate in the battle on July 3 but apparently did not keep a record of that event.

---

[25] David Trimble, Op. Cit., p. 26.

[26] Jean Muir Dorsey and Maxwell J. Dorsey, Op. Cit., p. 17.

By the time the French arrived at The Meadows, Washington and his men had built a small, circular palisade fort of rough hewn logs and had piled up dirt for some entrenchments. But it was an uneven match in many respects. On the English side were some 350 men from Virginia and South Carolina while the French commander, Louis Coulon de Villiers had approximately 750 regulars and Indians.

The marching, bad food and hard work had taken their toll on Washington's troops - making them near the point of exhaustion. Matters got worse when these bone-weary troops were beset with a heavy downpour throughout the day. Their entrenchments soon turned into a mudhole and their powder too damp to fire. With their cattle shot and with the dead and dying multiplying their prospects were indeed grim.

Toward sunset the beleaguered troops got a real surprise. Out of the woods came several French officers with a white flag asking for a parley. With about 100 of his men killed or wounded and with no expectations of relief, the young colonel saw no choice but surrender.

Taking his interpreter, Van Braam, Washington met in a downpour, under candle light, with his adversaries and worked out an honorable agreement. They were permitted to march away with honors of war and with each soldier allowed to keep personal possessions and a gun. This was quite generous when it is remembered that Louis was a brother of the French officer killed at the rocky glen.

Apparently unknown to Washington, there was a clause in the articles of capitulation which would turn out later to be a source of embarrassment. Van Braam had consented to allow the phrase "l 'assassinat de Jumonville" to be a part of the terms of surrender. This was tantamount to an admission that the French officer had been murdered rather than killed as an act of war. Needless to say, the French made the most of this as both sides sparred for diplomatic advantage. In any case, on July 4, Washington's battered and defeated troops vacated the Meadows and marched to Wills Creek.

Christopher was another big loser in this second confrontation near "The Forks." What the English didn't carry off to use against the French, the French carried away or burned on July 5 as they marched back to Fort Duquesne. He was financially ruined. Rubbing salt into an open wound, the Virginia legislature twice refused to award him any compensation.

Christopher returned to Wills Creek and then moved on to Winchester where he worked to supply Virginia troops as they prepared for a conflict which was certainly in the making. At this time the military planners in London were developing an overall strategy by which they would expel the French from North America. Christopher must have known that his knowledge of the frontier would be useful in this conflict but he could hardly have imagined being a guide for General Edward Braddock. This, however, was his fate.

Chapter V

Christopher Meets General Braddock

Christopher was appointed head guide by General Braddock in late May of 1755 while the combined British and Colonial forces were encamped in and around the newly built fort named to honor the Duke of Cumberland. Two of his sons, Nathaniel and Thomas, were also selected to serve as guides. He was joined here by George Washington who arrived with the general from Frederick Town, Maryland. They had escaped the perils of the journey to Fort Le Boeuf and now as fate would have it, they would survive even greater dangers in the service of a general who is reported to have looked with disdain on colonial wisdom.

Christopher was the logical choice for the position of guide to General Braddock. He was well acquainted with the route the army would take on its way to Fort Duquesne and well schooled in the habits of the French and Indians. Washington became a member of the general's staff as an unpaid volunteer who would serve as an aid. He had resigned his commission as a colonel in the Virginia forces sometime after returning from the battle of Fort Necessity because of a reorganization plan put into effect by Governor Robert Dinwiddie. By this proposal, Washington would have been reduced in rank to that of a captain. This, of course, was quite unacceptable to the ambitious young Virginian. His military career was advanced by acceptance as a member of Braddock's official family who were genuinely pleased to have his talents.

The march to Fort Duquesne was part of a grand strategy which included going up the Hudson River Valley toward Montreal and eventually subduing Quebec by entering the St. Lawrence River.

There were, of course, other military operations related to these major thrusts but we are primarily concerned with the expedition to get control of the "Forks."

Overall Strategy of the French and Indian War

General Braddock

The British government had determined that a major thrust against the French would be made in the spring of 1755. In pursuance of this objective, two regiments of British regulars were transported to North America. The Forty-fourth was to be under the command of Colonel Sir Peter Halkett while the Forty-eighth was to be led by Colonel Thomas Dunbar. These troops set sail from Cork, Ireland in January, 1755 and, after a stormy passage dropped anchor at Hampton Roads, Virginia.

Commodore Keppel had successfully piloted the squadron of some fifteen vessels safely to North America in preparation for a large campaign - with war still undeclared.[1]

After taking fresh provisions on board, the sea-weary army moved up the Chesapeake to Alexandria. There, after being further readied for the march, the army broke camp for Wills Creek. It was now April 10, 1755.

---

[1]Winthrop Sargent, The History of an Expedition Against Fort Duquesne, p. 141.

Braddock's March

Sir Peter Halkett, remaining on the Virginia side of the Potomac, made his way toward Winchester and then on to the upper Potomac. The next day Colonel Dunbar's regiment marched along the same road until they were opposite Rock Creek. They then crossed the Potomac into Maryland and marched to Frederick Town on their way to the mouth of"Conogogee" (now Conococheague Creek at the site of present day Williamsport, Maryland).

While encamped at Frederick Town, Braddock was joined by two notable Americans - Benjamin Franklin and George Washington - who, each in their own way would be of great service to the general. It was Franklin who would produce the sorely needed wagons for the army while the youthful aid would give counsel.

At dinner one evening, Franklin reports the following exchange with Braddock - an exchange which reveals the generals's naivete and self assuredness. Said Braddock,

> "I am to proceed to Niagra and having taken that, to Frontenac, if the season will allow time; and I suppose it will, for Duquesne can hardly detain me above three or four days; and then I can see nothing that will obstruct my march to Niagra."[2]

But Franklin's knowledge of the frontier brought a feeble attempt to caution the general about his unbounded optimism. There were obvious dangers in store for a European army, untrained in bush warfare, which would

---

[2]Lee McCardell, Ill-Starred General, p. 174.

be opposed by Indians with little or no regard for well lined troops and open-field maneuvers. He remarked to Braddock that,

> "The only danger I apprehend of obstruction to your march is from ambuscades of Indians, who by constant practice are dextrous in laying and executing them; and the slender line near four miles long, which your army must make, may expose it to be attacked by surprise in its flanks, and to be cut like a thread in several pieces . . . . "[3]

Braddock then, according to Franklin, brushed this caveat aside quickly with an impatient response that quieted the sage Pennsylvanian from further discussion,

> "The savages may indeed be a formidable enemy to your raw American militia, but upon the King's regulars and disciplined troops, Sir, it is impossible they should make any impression."[4]

Hard experience would teach the general otherwise abut the capabilities of "savages."

At Frederick town, General Braddock separated from Dunbar's regiment and in the company of Washington, crossed the Potomac River at Swearingen's Ferry - now Shepherdstown, West Virginia. They would visit Winchester for several days and then travel the same road as Sir Peter Halkett to Fort Cumberland.

Ahead of Dunbar were the Shennandoah or South mountains which contained several gaps through which his army could pass on the way to "Conogogee." Which pass or passes are still being debated and the record is not clear. An early historian of the area assets that it was Turner's gap which was used before crossing the Antietam at the "Devil's Back Bone."[5]

Finding the Potomac too low to use for water transport upstream, Dunbar crossed the Potomac and marched his troops to within a few miles of Winchester before turning northwest to Fort Cumberland. By the nineteenth of May, both regiments were encamped about the mouth of Wills Creek.

Braddock now had an imposing assembly of force. Each regiment of regulars had about 1000 men to which was added about 1200 provincials from several colonies and about 30 sailors from Commodore Keppel's fleet. They (sailors) were to supply skills in the use of block and tackle needed to move the heavy cannon over the steep mountain slopes.

On the day of battle, there were only 8 Indians with the British army in sharp contrast to over 600 Shawnees, Delawares, Ottawas and others in support of the French. Braddock's critics have regularly pointed out this failure. In actuality, some of the blame may be placed on his shoulders but some of the responsibility must be placed elsewhere. In any case, the badly needed intelligence which might have been provided by stealthy Indians was missing.

---

[3] Ibid., p. 174.

[4] Ibid., p. 175.

[5] Thomas J. C. Williams, History of Washington County, p. 39.

The loss is attributed to the general's inability to maintain good relations with even those Indians that did arrive at Fort Cumberland. He was perceived by Indians as haughty - looking down at them as too uncivilized for service to the British army. Also, there were conditions at the Fort which aggravated these feelings of hostility. Indian warriors were very resentful of the use of gifts and rum to seduce their women. As the situation deteriorated, Braddock ordered all Indian women to leave camp. When the braves followed, the army lost the major source of its' scouting capacity.

Another crippling blow to Indian support was not of the general's making. Contingents of Cherokees and Catawbas promised by Governor Dinwiddie failed to appear because of personal feuds of which he was unaware. While Braddock was on his way to America, Christopher went south to recruit warriors from these tribes. Braddock was at Fort Cumberland and the Indians promised had yet to appear. Something had to be done.

To speed up the process, Governor Dinwiddie sent Nathaniel Gist to prod the tardy Indians into action. It is reported that he had successfully engaged over four hundred warriors before some complications arose.

> ". . . Richard Pearis, a trader respected by the Indians, belittled the young man's efforts. He represented to them that Gist had no commission or presents and that one so young and of such little importance would not be sent on such a mission if their presence were greatly needed. Consequently Gist arrived at Fort Cumberland without the Indians."[6]

It has been surmised that Richard Pearis was striking out at the younger Gist because of a jealousy toward Christopher whose name had by now acquired some prominence.

It was not until May 29 that Braddock's army began its push toward its objective - Fort Duquesne. They now had the formidable task of cutting a twelve foot wide road the distance of about one hundred and ten miles. The intense labor required to clear trees and move boulders made it impossible at times to move forward more than three miles a day. Added to this was the weakened condition of the horses because of inadequate forage. They simply lacked the strength to pull the heavily loaded wagons and cannon up the steep grades. In late June, Washington was clearly impatient with the progress of the expedition. He wrote that the general had asked his opinion of the slow pace and that he". . . urged in the warmest terms I was able to push forward, if we even did it with a small but Chosen Band."[7] The proposal must have been agreeable to Braddock because at what is now known as Dunbar's Camp (near present Uniontown, Pennsylvania) and very near the site of the Jumonville encounter, he divided the army. Taking about 1500 of the fittest troops and only the most necessary supplies that could be carried by packhorse, the army moved on - leaving the remainder to follow at a slower pace.

On July 4, only five days before the fatal engagement, Christopher had a narrow escape. Captain Orme noted in his Journal the following story.

---

[6]Lawrence A. Orrill, Op. Cit., p. 209.

[7]W. W. Abbot (ed.) The Papers of George Washington, Vol. I, p. 321.

"From this place two of our Indians were prevailed upon to go for intelligence towards the French fort; and also (unknown to them), Gist, the General's guide:

The Indians returned on the 6th, and brought in a French officer's scalp, who was shooting within half a mile of the fort, and that they believed very few men were out upon observation. They saw some boats under the fort, and one with a white flag coming down the Ohio.

Gist returned a little after the same day, whose account corresponded with theirs, except he saw smoke in a valley between our camp and Du Quesne. He had concealed himself with an intent of getting close under the fort in the night, but was discovered and pursued by two Indians, who had very near taken him."[8]

As scouts, Christopher and his sons were exposed to constant danger. The French were always aware of the daily progress of Braddock's army. There were almost daily reports of Indians surprising stragglers or any who strayed too far from the main body. Those who were not scalped on the spot were captured and then subjected to unspeakable cruelties by their Indian captors.

As the army approached Turtle Creek, about eight miles from the Fort, a decision had to be made about the best approach. Near the creek, on the same side as the army, was a portion of land called the "Narrows" which, in addition to being a very likely place for an ambush, would be difficult to make passable without extreme labor. To circumvent the problem, Braddock made the choice to have his army ford the Monongahela upstream some eight miles and then ford it again downstream just below the mouth of Turtle Creek.

Very early on the morning of July 9, the advance troops secured the crossings and the army advanced as planned. Orders were given to march until 3 o'clock in the afternoon after all had crossed the second ford. After a night's rest, they would lay siege to the French stronghold. Accounts of the crossing stir the imagination. Full dress uniforms, martial music, flags and near precision marching through the shallow water were all intended to impress the French and excite the army.

By early afternoon the army had successfully crossed without incident and were lined up to resume the march. If unhindered, they would soon be placing their cannons at positions which would permit them to reduce the fort to splinters. There seemed to be no reason to doubt that this happy prospect was fully in the making since they had not been ambushed at the two most obvious places - the fordings.

Meanwhile, at the French fort, Captain Contrecoeur was well aware of the position of the oncoming British army. He was profoundly cognizant of his danger from the heavy guns carried at much expense in human and animal labor. He was clearly open to an honorable surrender or to an abandonment. But an unbelievable turn of events would alter this choice.

---

[8] WWinthrop Sargent, Op. Cit., p. 349.

Captain Daniel Beaujeu

At the pleadings of a handsome young French captain, Daniel de Beaujeu, Contrecoeur permitted about 250 officers, regulars and Canadians to volunteer to follow the bold plan to strike at Braddock on condition that they also win the support of an assortment of warriors from nearly a dozen Indian tribes encamped around the fort.

Fired by Beaujeu's enthusiasm, Delawares, Shawnees, Ottawas, Abenakis, Mingoes and others amassed a combination of over 600 warriors who were now ready to follow him against the enemy. They ran toward the oncoming army in a frenzy. What followed is on the order of the unbelievable - but it in fact happened.

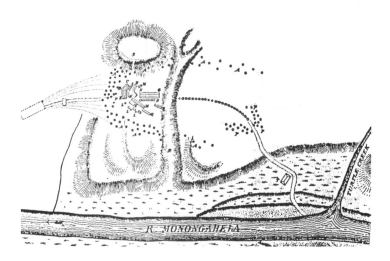

French Strategy at Turtle Creek[9]

About 1:30 p.m., on July 9, a collision occurred between the two converging armies. There was no ambush because Beaujeu could not effect such a plan in time. Upon impact the gallant young officer took a bullet to the head and was succeeded by Captain Dumas who must receive credit for what followed. Pressing on, the French and Indians made an enveloping maneuver which was to seal the fate of Braddock's army.

Working alongside the compacted British troops from behind the cover of trees they wrecked havoc at will. The vanguard fell back into the ranks of the oncoming main force which was at the same time being pressed forward by their officers - including Braddock. The result was a mass of red coats which made an easy target for French marksmen.

---

[9]Adapted from Francis Parkman, Montcalm and Wolfe, inside cover.

For some three hours, an unseen foe pumped round after round into an almost helpless foe. When a feeble attempt was made to break out and take a strategic hill to the right of the road, they were rebuffed, suffering more casualties from being shot in the back by their own men than from their obstinate enemy.

Braddock, it is clear, acquitted himself as regards personal courage. He had nearly a half dozen horses shot from under him before he received a fatal shot. Washington avers that he had no less than four bullet holes in his clothing. The carnage lasted until late afternoon with the resulting loss of 63 officers and 914 men either killed or wounded out of over 1,200 who entered the battle. The French lost a mere 16 and the Indians were reduced by only 27.

Not much is known about what Christopher and his sons did during the actual fighting. In all probability they fought with the Virginians who are reported to have handled themselves very well. One of the several journals that were kept gave a rather remarkable account of one incident involving Christopher. Known simply as "British B" and regarded as of questionable authenticity his story is reproduced as follows:

> ". . . I shall give you the particulars of Sir Peter Halkett's death. Just after he had left the general, as I have above related, he rode to the head of his men and riding about to give necessary orders, he was observed by an Indian fellow, who sat disabled in the field by a shot in his knee; this savage leveled his piece at Sir Peter as he rode about, which one Capt. Ghist, a Capt. of the Militia and huntsman perceiving who had just discharged his musket, he made haste to reload, in order to prevent the danger with which Sr. Peter was threatened, but could not make such dispatch but that the Indian had shot Sir Peter down, before he was in readiness to oppose him. Ghist however immediately step'd up and blew out the miscreant's brains."[10]

Mercifully, in late afternoon, the call for retreat was given. Those who were still able plunged headlong back across the Monongahela and raced in fear towards Dunbar's Camp. Afterwards they made a hasty retreat to Fort Cumberland. The wounded general was carried on a litter to within a few miles of Fort Necessity where he died. His remains were deliberately placed where troops and wagons would obliterate any signs of a grave and preclude the possibility of desecration by Indians. It would be three years before a British army would again attempt to capture Fort Duquesne.

Braddock has had many defenders and critics. It is not necessary to record these ad infinitum. But it is worthwhile to set the general's reputation alongside of his guide to show how they have fared in time. Another guide, the Oneida Chief, Scarouady, was of this opinion.

> "It was the pride and ignorance of that general that came from England. He looked upon us as dogs, and would never hear anything what was said to him. We often tried to tell him of the danger he was in with his soldiers, but he never appeared pleased with us, and that was the reason that a great many of our warriors left him and would not be under his command."[11]

Surely this was an important contribution to the humiliating defeat at Turtle Creek. There is no record of how much advice Christopher ever gave - or if given - how much was accepted.

---

[10]Paul E. Kopperman, Braddock at The Monongahela, p. 172.

[11]Lee McCardell, Op. Cit., p. 263.

Christopher emerged from the battle with his reputation more intact than Braddock. A letter from the Department of Internal Affairs in Harrisburg certifies the following commendation.

> "This is to certify that Mr. Christopher Gist executed the Office of head guide with great Sobriety Prudence & Fidelity to which Office he was appointed by Gen'l Braddock the 27th of May 1755. And I do farther certify that he was sent to bring intelligence from the French Fort which service he performed with great Risk being for a long time pursued. Upon his return the Gen'l being very well satisfied with his behavior ordered Mr. Shirley the Secretary to pay him 50 thirty six Shilling Pieces."[12]

Returning once more to the immediate events after the retreat, we come upon another disaster. Colonel Dunbar, who was now in command, was seized with panic along with the troops. He was most zealous in the destruction of all war materials that could not be carted or carried away. Upon reaching Fort Cumberland, he hastily marched his troops to Philadelphia for "winter" quarters - leaving the whole frontier exposed to French and Indian depredation.

It has often been pointed ut that he might well have regrouped and marched back to the Fort for an almost certain victory. The Indians would have been in no condition to fight because they were more interested in scalping the dead and near dead and in looting the battlefield. Further, they quickly overindulged in the rum they had uncovered and became incapacitated for battle due to drunkenness.

Attention has also been given to the fact that Dunbar was tardy to the point of embarrassment in keeping up with the advance army but was the embodiment of efficiency in retreat.

Washington summed up the campaign failure succinctly in a letter to a friend.

> "I join heartily with you in believing that when this story comes to be related in future Annals, it will meet with unbelief and indignation; for had I not been witness to the fact on that fatal Day, I sh'd scarce have given credit to it even now."[13]

After the battle, both Christopher and Washington returned to Virginia to make what defenses they could against the barbarian onslaught that would not be long in coming. Numerous reports of the day repeat the extent of the devastation. Captain Dumas, who replaced the forces bragged that he had,

> ". . . succeeded in ruining the three adjacent provinces of Pennsylvania, Maryland and Virginia, driving off the inhabitants, and totally destroying the settlements over a tract of country thirty leagues wide reckoning from the line of Fort Cumberland . . . . The enemy has lost far more since the battle than on the day of his defeat."[14]

---

[12] Jean Muir Dorsey and Maxwell J. Dorsey, Op. Cit., p. 18.

[13] W. W. Abbot (ed.), Op. Cit., p. 350.

[14] Francis Parkman, Op. Cit., pps. 192-93.

Colonel Adam Stephen wrote to Washington from Fort Cumberland that,

> "The Smoak of Burning Plantations darken the day and hide the neighboring mountains from our Sight."[15]

Father Claude Godfroy, a priest, wrote from Quebec to his brother that,

> "The Indians do not take any prisoners; they kill all they meet, men, women and children. Every day they have some for their kettles, and after having abused the women and maidens, they slaughter or burn them."[16]

Similar reports abound coming from a frontier area which stretched over four hundred miles. It would take three years of defensive fort building and troop training before another offensive campaign could be made.

Soon after returning to Virginia, Washington was commissioned a colonel and made commander in chief of the Virginia forces. Christopher returned to his home at Opeekon, near Winchester. After doing some duties as a messenger and a commissary agent for the government of Virginia, he was given the commission of captain in charge of a company of scouts. The two veterans of the trail and the campaign would now be working in the defense of Virginia.

---

[15]W. W. Abbot (ed.), Vol II, p. 12.

[16]Walter O'Meara, Guns at The Forks, p. 161.

Chapter VI

From Commissary to Captain

Christopher 's natural ability to do many things will at this point in his life be the source of problems - some of which he does not appear to have managed very well. In addition to being a scout, he was called upon to recruit troops, carry important messages, train scouts and act as commissary.
As early as 1754. He was an assistant to John Carlyle who was in charge of acquiring food, uniforms and other supplies for the expedition to the "Forks".

It was in the capacity of assistant supply agent that Christopher faced some of his most trying times. Until October 10, 1755, when he received his captaincy, Christopher was involved in the procurement of supplies along with his other duties. The skills required of a scout were of a different order from those needed by a purchasing agent and the inadequate concern for detail incubated serious misunderstandings.

The many interruptions in record keeping brought about by absences for lengthy periods of time would of itself preclude accuracy in the recording and transfer of goods. These lapses would lead some to make charges of corruption and even embezzlement[1] by the governor of Maryland.

Even those charges which may have some appearance of legitimacy will, upon further investigation, not be the result of willful dishonesty. This claim is warranted because, without exception, his immediate superiors gave him unqualified support when Christopher's integrity was at issue.

The questioning began as the result of an inspection tour on the part of Governor Horatio Sharpe of Maryland who made a visit to the newly built fort at Wills Creek. This was to be named Fort Cumberland by General Braddock when he arrived there in May of 1755. Sharpe made his appearance in November, 1754 and found a good many things not to his liking. All of his complaints were outlined in a lengthy letter to Governor Robert Dinwiddie of Virginia. Governor Sharpe first ordered another fort to be built on a higher elevation just behind the one he found objectionable because of its small size. He then described the Governor Horatio Sharpe unsatisfactory situation regarding
supplies for the troops and purposed several measures that would, in his opinion, improve the management of the fort's provisions. His first recommendation was:

---

[1]Paul H. Giddens, "The French and Indian War in Maryland," Maryland Historical Magazine, p. 295.

Governor Horatio Sharpe

"to appoint a Commissary of Reputation Ability and some fortune who with the assistance of a Deputy & a Clerk will be able to attend & execute that Business in a proper & satisfactory manner. His Clerk always & himself for the most part to be resident in the magazine at Wills Creek to receive Cure & deliver the Provisions"[2]

Both of these suggestions, if they were to become policy, would have disqualified Christopher for that position.

Sharpe's next recommendation was to remedy the chronic shortage of salt which was needed for curing meat. In the absence of salt, the cattle could not be butchered and the meat cured and stored for future use. They were left to forage in the woods under the watchful eyes of hired herdsmen. The cost must have been very high but since Christopher had promised payment, the governor reluctantly paid the bill so that public faith in Maryland's credit would not be impaired. Aside from the fact that the governor was irritated at the management practices he saw, it became clear that he also did not trust Christopher. Going beyond mere criticism of his ability as a commissary agent, Sharpe informed Dinwiddie that he,

"was importuned also a good Deal by Mr Gists Creditors with some of whom I am indeed somewhat suspicious that he has hardly acted the honest part; wherefore I would beg the favor of you to signify to me what sums were advanced to him when he was at Williamsburg & for what uses that I may examine whether all the Complaints against him are without foundation. I was told that He did receive several Sums of Money of you to discharge a good many Debts but that instead of appropriating it in that manner He paid off with part thereof some old Debts that he had contracted on his own private Account & with the Remainder purchased a Quantity of Goods to trade with also on his own account"[3]

It is possible that extenuating circumstance made it necessary to stall creditors and juggle funds to keep them all satisfied to some degree. Also, it should be remembered that Christopher's personal fortune was at low ebb because the French had just destroyed everything at the new settlement. While this would not justify fraud, it might be the basis of some shifting that might be within the limits of tolerance.

But Governor Sharpe had more to complain about. He claimed that Andrew Montour, the Indian interpreter, was very agitated because Christopher had not paid him £45 which had been entrusted to him to deliver. The matter was somewhat cleared up when Governor Dinwiddie replied to

---

Horatio Sharpe, Correspondence, p. 137.

Ibid., p. 139.

"Mr Gist rec^d £45 to pay Mr Montour, but by the acct sent appears he paid him only £20 what other monies he had was from Carlyle to pay for Cattle purchased the particular Sum I know not. M^r . Montour's Account is very unfair, he had no orders to raise the Men charged. . . ."[4]

The discrepancy now appears to be partly in the different accounting which now indicated that Christopher had paid Montour about half of the money. Again, there should be no rush to judgement. It is hard to believe that Christopher would be dishonest toward someone with whom he had shared so much that was dependent upon mutual trust.

Further, he would surely need the friendship and trust of one of the most influential Indians of the day. He could ill afford to estrange a figure so important to his own future in all dealings with other Indians. In the absence of knowing more about their personal financial transactions, it is hasty to assume the worst.

Governor Dinwiddie's response did not satisfy Governor Sharpe. The matter dragged on for months. Then Sharpe concluded the issue bluntly by asserting that the whole episode "gives me the greatest Reason to believe he deals unfairly & has been guilty of an Embezzlement."[5]

William Fairfax, the Virginia baron, came to Christopher's defense. He quickly drafted a letter to Governor Dinwiddie assuring him of the integrity of both Christopher and his superior. Dinwiddie promptly replied that he, ". . . always had and have a good opinion of Mr. Gist's Capacity and Integrity yet I did not think him a proper person to Act as Commissary to the forces"[6]

This qualified support, however, serves to indicate that Christopher may have been badly placed in the function of a supply agent. In this regard, he was not alone. The reports of other commissary agents abound with instances of delays, spoiled meat, mouldy flour and overall mismanagement.

With the coming of Braddock to America, Christopher's services would be sorely needed in an area where he was demonstrably more skilled - that of scout. This has been noted and we need to take into account the new demands made of him because of Braddock's defeat.

It will be recalled that Colonel Dunbar hastily exited Fort Cumberland in August for "winter" quarters in Philadelphia. This, of course, left the whole frontier exposed to French and Indian incursions on frontier settlements. The extent of the devastation has already been related - but it is not to be forgotten that war has yet to be declared and that it will continue for seven years after the formal declaration. In preparation for the defense of the colony of Virginia, Governor Dinwiddie became involved in a number of activities - all calculated to avert disaster.

Eventually a plan for a series of forts emerged with Washington charged with the responsibility to construct. Using Fort Loudoun at Winchester as his base of operation, the young commander-in-chief began the enormous task.

---

[4] Ibid., p. 144.

[5] Ibid., p. 226.

[6] Kenneth P. Bailey, Op. Cit., p. 101.

Forts Planned for the Defense of Virginia[7]

At this juncture, the leaders of the Virginia forces needed vital information in order to know what direction their preparations should take. It was natural that Christopher would be called upon to journey into Pennsylvania during the fall of 1755 to obtain the intelligence needed to plan for an effective defense.

His orders from Washington included the request that he use his "utmost endeavors to engage them [Indians] to come and lodge their Wives and Families in our Forts and assist us in fighting their own battles."[8]   He was also empowered to offer Andrew Montour, the well respected Indian interpreter, a captain's commission if he would raise a company (sixty) of Indians to fight with the Virginia Regiment.

Christopher reported the progress of his trip to Washington in a letter dated October 15, 1755.[9] Following are some of the more significant points in the letter: First, Colonel Dunbar was now on his way toward New York, Therefore, there could be no return to retake Fort Duquesne. Christopher apparently could not resist the temptation to comment on the widespread dislike for Colonel Dunbar because of his hasty retreat.

He flattered Washington by telling him he was "more talked off in Pennsylvania then any other person." Pennsylvania also had plans to recruit southern Indians and Christopher wrote that he fully expected to be pressed by them "to Get the Cattawbees Indians . . . and the Cherokees in the Spring." Finally, he noted that Washington was in dire need of blankets, stockings and shoes and asked for help from the leaders of Pennsylvania.

---

[7] Douglas Southall Freeman, George Washington, p. 229.

[8] W. W. Abbot (ed.), Op. Cit., Vol. II, p. 125.

[9] Ibid., pps. 114-15.

There was also a great need to find out from Indian leaders what their intentions were as the great powers lined up for conflict. Would they be neutral? Could they be won over to the French cause? Could they be induced by some means to supply warriors in support of the English cause? To find out the state of affairs on these questions and to recruit men, Christopher was again on horseback to Philadelphia.

On November 1, Christopher wrote to Washington informing him of events in Pennsylvania. He would be meeting with Monacatootha and the other chiefs at John Harris's Ferry to discern their intentions. Christopher must have earned a substantial reputation there because he mentioned to Washington that Governor Morris had offered him a captain's commission in the military forces of that colony. He turned down the offer because he had been informed only two weeks earlier that he had a similar offer from Virginia. There was, of course, no reason for Washington to doubt Christopher's word about the offer from Pennsylvania. Shortly thereafter (October 31), Washington received a letter from the governor of Pennsylvania in which he paid high tribute to the scout from Virginia. He wrote,

> "Good Intelligence being of the utmost Consequences at this Juncture, and Mr. Gist knowing more of Indians and of the Nature of the Country than any other Man here I have availed myself of his coming and desired him to go by Mr. Weisers & consult with him in what manner to obtain true Accots of the Motions of the Enemy."[10]

It was indeed encouraging to see that Pennsylvania, after much delay, was now on the move - even to the point of appropriating money for the defense of its border. As Christopher put it in his last letter, "They intend to do Something in Arnest."[11]

Returning to Christopher's appointment, we learn something of the interest Washington had in the wellbeing of the older scout-turned-soldier. On October 10, Washington wrote to Christopher informing him of the appointment to a captaincy of a company of scouts - one of seventeen planned for the Virginia Regiment. It was the only commission left unfilled and it required "earnest solicitation" on the part of Washington to get it. The commission was, ". . . attended with equal Honor, Rank and Profit with the other Captains; but will be accompanied with more Fatigue."[12]

Christopher began recruiting to fill his company without delay. While on the second trip to Pennsylvania he met with success and informed Washington that,

> "I have Sent twenty of My Soldiers to York Town who are all in good Sperritts there and two I now Send to them. To Morrow I shall follow them I have been forced to Borrow Money and if Could have had Money enough I Believe I should have had 50 Men by this time."[13]

---

[10] Ibid., p. 151.

[11] Ibid., p. 154.

[12] Ibid., p. 98.

[13] Ibid., p. 180.

The new captain was expected to be in Winchester with a complete company by late December. But because he and his son Nathaniel, who had now been commissioned a lieutenant in his father's company, were so successful at recruiting they were ordered to continue this work. Washington wrote to them with the order to "proceed to those public Places where you have the greatest probability of success, and continue Recruiting until the first day of March."[14]

The two recruiters were forbidden to enlist any apprentices or indentured servants because their masters complained loudly about financial losses. This did not seem to deter all recruiters because they were paid a per-head bounty. In March they returned to Winchester to resume their duties as scouts. They had to plead mightily to the governor to reimburse them for money they had spent out of their own pockets.

A look at the roll for Christopher's Company for July 13, 1756 shows that he had sixty-eight men - recruited mostly from Pennsylvania, Maryland and Virginia. Most of them were in their early twenties and short of stature. Only four were six feet in height while the average was about 5 feet-seven inches tall. Since few could sign their names, they were identified by physical descriptions such as "dark," "fair," "well set," "fresh colored," "raw boned," "tender eyed," "thin," "spare," "red haired" and "lusty."[15]

Christopher was a captain of this company of scouts for over a year and a half before it was disbanded in June, 1757. During this time the unit was stationed for varying periods of time at Fort Loudoun (Winchester), Fort Cumberland (Wills Creek) and Maidstone - also referred to as "Conegocheeg" by writers of the day. From his letters to Washington, it is clear that he faced the usual trials and tribulations endemic to frontier forts.

Christopher reported that he was having problems with deserters and that he was still uncompensated for personal expenditures used for recruiting. Washington quickly wrote to Governor Dinwiddie on his behalf, pleading for a quick settlement of the unpaid bill.

> "I doubt not your Honor will consider the justice of them [claims], and assist the poor man in the affair as he is put to great inconvenience for want of money, has been obliged to advance his own, as far as it would go, and people to whom he owes balances upon that account are daily threatening him with suits."[16]

Not taking any chances that the governor might fail to act promptly, Washington penned another letter the very next day to John Robinson, Speaker of the House of Burgesses for the colony of Virginia, to use his influence to correct the deficit.

> "Captain Gist also has diverse times entreated me, in the most interesting manner to intercede in his behalf, that he may get the balance of his accoupt; his distress calling aloud for all the assistance that these sums can contribute.

---

[14]Ibid., p. 247.

[15]Lloyd DeWitt Bockstruck, Virginia's Colonial Soldier, pps. 68-71.

[16]W. W. Abbot (ed.), Op. Cit., Vol. II, p. 315.

I do not know really, who to apply to for this purpose, or whose right it is to pay the Accompt, but is certainly wrong not to pay him at all. If a hearty zeal for the interest of this Colony - many losses in serving it - and true distress can recommend him to any favor, he certainly merits indulgence."[17]

Earlier it was pointed out that Christopher and his company of scouts were subjected to a host of problems associated with life at a frontier post and that as a consequence there was much desertion from the army. The most common afflictions were scurvy, small pox, dysentery or "bloody flux," boredom, cruel and inhuman punishment, a very limited diet, low pay, constant association with the lower ranks of society and very little female companionship. Such an imposing list of deficiencies was bound to produce desertion as a means of escape.

Camp conditions, with the usual unconcern for cleanliness, was conducive to the spread of germs. Lack of vegetables accounted for the scurvy. The allowance of only four to eight women per company was bound to result in boredom and loneliness. Enlisted men were recruited from the "riff-raff" of society who brought with them a propensity for drinking, fighting and other habits which attracted discipline. The universal reaction of officers was the infliction of severe penalties.

In this regard, Washington was as prone to severity as other officers of his day. His reports of disciplinary action, including lashing, are similar to those from all frontier forts. These reports make one cringe, as they read. On May 1, 1756, Washington issued the following order at Fort Loudoun.

"Any Soldier, who shall presume to quarrel or fight shall receive five hundred lashes, without the benefit of a Court Martial. The Offender upon complaint made shall have strict justice done. Any Soldier found drunk, shall immediately receive one hundred lashes; without Benefit of a Court Martial[18]

Soon thereafter, Washington wrote to Governor Dinwiddie requesting his

approval of a death sentence for desertion a second time on the part of an

enlisted man.

"I enclose your Honor the Sentence of a General Court Martial, which was held here upon a Sergeant for running away with his Party. They have, I think very justly adjudged him to suffer Death; which sentence I hope you approve of; as there never was a fitter object to make an Example of - being the second time he has been guilty of the same crime"[19]

The governor apparently agreed with Washington's sentence because he wasted no time in issuing the death warrant. He then reaffirmed the logic of severity

---

[17]Ibid., p. 325.

[18]W. W. Abbot (ed.), Op. Cit., Vol. III, p. 70.

[19]Ibid., p. 84.

in declaring, "that he may be a public Example to deter others from such Offenses"[20]

In another case, Washington informed Dinwiddie of a double hanging that had already taken place. "Setting an example" was again used as the rationale.

> "I send Your Honor a copy of the proceedings of a General Court Martial. Two of those condemned, namely Ignatious Edwards and Wm Smith, were hanged on Thursday last, just before the Companies marches for their respective posts. Your Honor will, I hope excuse my hanging, instead of shooting them, It Conveyed much more terror to others; and it was for examples sake, we did it . . . ."[21]

But severity did not deter desertions. They continued throughout the war. It is possible that serving under Braddock had a strong influence upon Washington. The General's Orderly Book - surely available to Washington - gives a model of the day. Several instances from this source will illustrate the normal character for that day of what is now called cruel and inhuman treatment. "Any Soldier who shall desert tho' he return again will be hanged without mercy."[22] Again, "Any Soldier by leaving his company, or by words or Gestures expressing Fear shall suffer death . . . ."[23]

Reports of court martial sentencing give vivid evidence of extreme punishments. At Alexandria where the army readied for the expedition there was cruel punishment and this continued throughout the campaign. The Log contains the following entry.

> "The General Court Martial whereof Lieut. Colo. Gage was President is dissolv'd, and James Anderson of Colo Dunbar's Regiment who was tryed by ye General Court Martial is ordered 1000 lashes with a Cat and Nine tails. . . ."[24]

Sometimes these lashings were stretched out over several days because the prisoners were unconscious or bleeding so badly that further punishment would have killed them. Sentences of such uncommon harshness were routine at this time.

At Fort Cumberland, three men stole a keg of beer. For this offense they were given the following sentence: Thomas Conelly, one thousand lashes; Jas Fitzgerald, eight hundred lashes and Jas Hughes, eight hundred lashes. It was later decided to reduce the number and Conelly was awarded three hundred three different times while the other culprits were each given six hundred at two separate lashings.[25]

---

[20]Ibid., p. 103.

[21]W. W. Abbot (ed.), Op. Cit., Vol. IV, p. 360.

[22]Will H. Lowdermilk, History of Cumberland, Maryland, Appendix p. V.

[23]Ibid., p. VIII.

[24]Ibid., p. XII.

[25]Ibid., p. XXXIV.

There is no need to extend the number of examples. The Orderly Book is a showcase of inhumanity. Gambling, drunkenness and other infractions were quickly dealt with by the ever-ready whip which probably induced more fear than Indians. Camp discipline was also a part of Christopher's experience as a captain of a company of scouts.

But Christopher's days as a scout were numbered. The cost of maintaining a large number of troops and supplying presents to the Indian allies was a drain upon the treasury of the Colony of Virginia. In an effort to reduce the costs of defense, the number of companies was reduced from seventeen to ten in May, 1757. Those captains whose companies were disbanded were then asked to accept a demotion to the rank of lieutenant. Only Christopher agreed to such a reduction in rank and pay.

But it was of little consequence. Soon after the demotion, Christopher resigned his post in the Virginia Regiment to take the post of Deputy of Indian Affairs for the southern district. He was now fifty-two years of age and undoubtedly interested in a more settled occupation than the rigors of the trail or scouting for the army.

In the new position he would be able to bring his experiences of the trail, the scout and the soldier to bear on the delicate task of lining up the Indians on the British side. His maturity of years and his knowledge of Indian ways would be of incalculable service as the war dragged on.

It is possible to assess the relative importance of Christopher's appointment by looking at what is going on at the same time in the Northern Department of Indian Affairs. At the head of the department was the colorful - but very able - Sir William Johnson, who kept the Six Nations aligned with the British interests. He appointed as his deputy assistant the very qualified Indian trader, George Croghan. It is hard to imagine a more powerful, able and respected duo than these two men. That Christopher was in such company was a tribute to his capabilities. Keeping the Indians friendly or at least neutral was key strategy for winning the war. Both men gave much and achieved much.

A backward look at Christopher's success as a captain of scouts is more complimentary of his talents than that of commissary. There are numerous reports of Indians on scalping raids within the vicinity of Winchester although most were to the north and west of the town. The fact that Indians approached the area with much caution indicated that Virginia's emerging defense system was becoming more effective. Christopher undoubtedly engaged in some of these skirmishes.

Nathaniel, Christopher's oldest son, is known to have had at least one harrowing encounter with the French. In May, 1756, while on a scouting venture out of Fort Cumberland with Colonel Cresap, their party had a brisk engagement along the Youghiogheny River.

> "After going some distance, Cresap's men mutinied, whereupon Gist and his men left them and proceeded alone. At a point on Laurel Hill, back of Connellsville, they met a number of French and Indians from Fort Duquesne on a similar mission to the Virginia frontier. There followed a sharp skirmish, which lasted for almost an hour, the Virginians losing two men and the French six. Gist, having reason to believe that a greater number of enemy were coming up from the crossing, brought off his men with great skill and after

some difficulty returned to Fort Cumberland, where he was given credit for unusual courage."[26]

It must have been gratifying for Christopher to see his sons engaged in a cause to which he was dedicated. They would continue in their work as soldiers while their father prepared for the duty of recruiting Indians for service against their French antagonists.

---

[26]Lawrence A. Orrill, Op. Cit., p. 212.

Chapter VII

Christopher Becomes Deputy Agent of Indian Affairs

In the spring of 1756 the position of Deputy Agent of Indian Affairs of the Southern Department became vacant because Edmond Atkin was promoted from that position to be the new superintendent. Washington suggested that Christopher be given the newly vacant post not only because he wanted to be relieved of the worries attendant with management of Indian affairs but because he was well aware of the older scout's knowledge of Indians and their ways.

On May 30, Washington wrote a letter to Governor Robert Dinwiddie complaining of the management of Indian affairs and pointed out the need for one person "of good sense and probity," to supervise affairs with the various Indian tribes. According to Washington,

> "An Indian will never forget a promise made to him: They are naturally suspicious, and if they meet with delays, or disappointments, in their expectations; will scarcely ever be reconciled. For which reason, nothing ought ever to be promised but what is performed; and one only person be empowered to do either. If Your Honor shou'd think this an advisable measure, and be inclined to carry it into execution, I would beg leave to recommend Mr. Gist as the most proper person I am acquainted with to conduct the Business. He knows but little of their language it is true; but is well acquainted with their manners and customs - especially of the Southern Indians. And, for his honesty and zeal I think I dare vouch.[1]

This expression of confidence came after almost four years of acquaintance with the trail-worn scout and in spite of assertions to the contrary from other sources.

Washington did not waste time in using his influence to secure the open position for his friend. On the very same day he wrote another letter to John Robinson, Speaker of the House of Burgesses, with the following observation,

> "The French, Sir, have a proper person appointed to the direction of these affairs; who makes it his sole business to study their dispositions, and the art of pleasing them. This person is invested with power to treat with, and reward them for every piece of service; and by timely presents, on suitable occasions, obtain very great advantages. . . . And I know of no person so well qualified for an undertaking of this sort as the Bearer, Captain Gist. He has had extensive dealings with the Indians, is in great esteem among them; well acquainted with their manners and customs - is indefatigable and patient: most excellent

---

[1]W. W. Abbot (ed.) The Papers of George Washington, Vol IV, p. 172.

qualities indeed, where Indians are concerned! And, for his capacity, honesty and zeal, I dare venture to engage."[2]

Such unbounded assurances was sure to work in Christopher's favor. On July 25, 1757, he was appointed deputy by Edmond Atkin. The appointment was confirmed by Governor Dinwiddie on October 24 with the following instructions.

"You are to take care of the Goods appointed for Indian presents in the same Method as done by Mr. Atkin . . . . And I shall be glad when any Indians come in, that you keep them out of the Town or dispatch them immediately on duty, as I am convinced they are very unruly when they get a Liquor."[3]

Early in the new year of 1758, Christopher took up residence in the town of Winchester. In all probability his daughter Anne was there as well as his sons. His first duties involved the many details of taking over a new job: taking stock of Indian presents on hand, determining what presents would be needed to assure a large supply of Indians for the upcoming Forbes campaign and getting several assistants to help with the work.

When Christopher was notified of his appointment by Superintendent Atkin, he also received a lengthy set of instructions detailing his duties. First was a request for a quarterly report of presents awarded to Indians and an inventory of presents on hand. This would make it possible to have a steady supply of goods to keep the Indians happy. They usually took to their heels for home if no presents were on hand to pay for their services.

The second demand was intended to stop Indian disturbances such as drunken quarrels and fracases resulting from the theft of horses from settlers as the warriors traveled to and from their homes in the Carolinas to scouting sites on the frontier. Atkin asked that Indian scouting parties be escorted along the far western fringe of Virginia by more isolated trails.

To standardize the treatment of Indians and avoid petty jealousies a bounty was set.

". . . a reward of £45 is allowed to any Indian in Amity with the Inhabitants of this Colony for every Indian Enemy taken Prisoner by him, & a Reward of £40 also for every Indian Enemy killed or destroyed; which Rewards, in Case the present Hostilities shall cease within two years. . . ."[4]

A bounty upon scalps however introduced temptations on the part of Indians to which Christopher must be on guard.

". . . The killing or destroying them can seldom be proved but by Scalps, of which the Cherokees in particular have found the art of making four out of one Enemy killed, & being unwilling, from a Puncto of Honour, to deliver them up at any rate they have it in their Power to produce the same again, so that a

---

[2] Ibid., pp. 174-75.

[3] Jean Muir Dorsey and Maxwell Jay Dorsey, Christopher Gist of Maryland and Some of His Descendants, p. 25. (From Official Records of Robert Dinwiddie, Vol. II, pp. 708-9.)

[4] Kenneth P. Bailey, Christopher Gist, p. 212.

wide Door is open thereby to fraud or Imposition & consequently great expense."[5]

There were several other requests imposed upon Christopher which were in the form of advice. Superintendent Atkin was knowledgeable about Indian habits and manners and was not reserved about sharing his expertise.

It is interesting to browse over the list of items to be used as presents to entice the southern Indians to scout and fight on the British side. There were guns, scalping knives, blankets, tomahawks, calico cloth for Indian women, coats, brass kettles, silver broaches, vermillion (red) warpaint, wampum and silver gorgets, to mention only a few.[6] These articles were held in high esteem by Indians and were successfully used by both sides to court the favor of native Americans.

As the British forces began to gear up for the second attempt to take Fort Duquesne, the need to keep relationships with the various Indian tribes on good terms became increasingly important. The leadership did not want a repeat of the Braddock calamity which, in part, was due to a lack of Indian support. A major part of Christopher's work in 1758 was that of maintaining good will and recruiting Indians for service. This would be an endurance contest.

Brigadier General John Forbes was picked to lead the expedition against Fort Duquesne. His army consisted of about 3000 provincials from Maryland, Pennsylvania and the Carolinas. In addition, there were some 1600 regulars of the Royal American Regiment. Finally, there were to be several hundred southern Indians - mostly recruited from the Cherokee and Catawba tribes. It is not clear how many Indians actually took part in the fighting because of the turnover in attendance.

The expedition was not only slow in getting started, it was dangerously slow in reaching its objective. The Fort was successfully taken on November 24 - very late in the season - in an era when most campaigns were over in July or August. General Forbes was dependent upon a very able Swiss mercenary, Colonel Henry Bouquet, because throughout the campaign he was incapacitated by the "bloody flux."

As the army worked its way westward from Carlisle, a serious debate erupted over the route to be taken. Many, including Washington, had assumed that at some point, possibly Bedford, the army would drop southward and pick up on the old road cut by Braddock. But General Forbes and Colonel Bouquet had an all Pennsylvania passage in mind. This, of course, meant cutting a new road all the way - even across Laurel Mountain - which many thought impossible.

---

[5] Ibid., p. 212.

[6] Ibid., pp. 200-204.

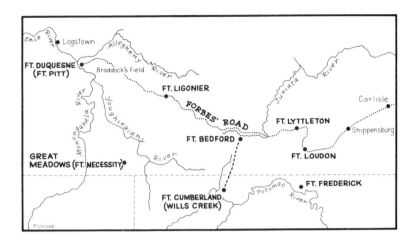

Forbes Route to Fort Duquesne - 1758

There may well have been political and economic motives under the surface of the debate which both sides did not admit openly - namely, that the colony with a well established road to the west would be well ahead of other colonies in settlement and trade. Both parties to the debate gave assurances that only military considerations entered into their judgments.

Washington was alarmed at the decision not to use a road that was already laid out. Expressing such fears, he wrote to Colonel Bouquet in July, 1758.

> ". . . I am convinced that a road, to be compared with General Braddock's or, indeed that will be fit for transportation even by pack-horses, cannot be made. . . I have uniformly told that, if you expect a tolerable road by Raystown you will be disappointed for no movement can be made that way without destroying our horses."[7]

But letters and heated discussions failed to move his superiors from their position.

Washington was not easily discouraged from his strongly held opinion. He next wrote a letter to a friend which eventually resulted in a nasty reprimand from Forbes and Bouquet. The friend, Major Francis Halkett, happened to be an aide de damp to General Forbes who allowed the letter to become known to the general. The letter expressed forcefully the opinion that,

> "If Colonel Bouquet succeeds in this point with the General all is lost! All is lost by Heavens! Our enterprise is ruined ". . . .[8]

---

[7]Will H. Lowdermilk, History of Cumberland, pps. 238-39.

[8]Walter O'Meara, Op. Cit. p. 186.

The General appears to have regarded Washington's opinion as representing the Virginia interest and not a military judgement. When it became clear that he had lost the argument, Washington dropped the subject.

The army trudged its way mile by mile and tree by tree, winding its way through the Pennsylvania mountains. By September they were encamped at Raystown - the site of Fort Bedford. Ahead was Laurel Hill which was an imposing ridge indeed. Sheer willpower and dogged strength brought about a successful crossing and by November the 2nd the army was camped on the Loyalhannon Creek where Fort Ligonier was built. They were now about 50 miles from their objective.

Although the season for campaigning was usually over by this time, Colonel Bouquet had not yet decided to halt operations. In an uncharacteristic move, Colonel Bouquet was persuaded by a younger officer, Major James Grant, to undertake a scouting expedition with about 800 men to the very confines of Fort Duquesne. After several tactical blunders, Grant's forces were routed - resulting in heavy loses. The toll for the disaster was 273 men killed, wounded or missing.

One of the missing troops at the memorable battle on "Grant's Hill" was Ensign Thomas Gist. He was wounded and carried away to Canada by his captors. Luckily he was able to escape and after a year of much hardship, found his way back to Virginia.[9]

The survivors of the Grant debacle made their way back to Fort Ligonier and rejoined the main forces. The situation was now getting desperate. Steady rains brought about swollen streams and much mud, making the roads unusable. To be snow-bound in such an advanced position without adequate supplies could bring on another loss to rival that of Braddock's.

Fortunately, three prisoners just captured gave intelligence abut the conditions at the French fort. Not only was there a much smaller number of troops than they had supposed but their Indian allies had left for home. General Forbes, with Colonel Bouquet's concurrence, then made the daring decision to press on. On November 24, as the British army neared their goal, they head a thundering blast. The French had exploded the magazine and torched the buildings. The next day Bouquet's troops entered the ruined fort, raised the British flag and renamed the site Fort Pitt. One of those who took over the abandoned fort was the eldest son of Christopher Gist - Nathaniel.[10] Endurance had paid off. The fortunes of war would now turn in favor England - eventuating in the expulsion of the French from North America.

Returning to the work of recruitment by Christopher, it is now possible to assess its impact upon the Forbes campaign. Indians began to arrive at Winchester as early as April, 1758. It is estimated that about 650 (mostly Cherokees) were in the area by May. More would have been present but for the excessive heat - a novel excuse for delay.[11]

Cost aside, the Indians became a real nuisance as the campaign in Pennsylvania dragged on. Inactivity brought on restlessness. While waiting for

---

[9]Lawrence A. Orrill, Op. Cit. p. 215.

[10]Ibid. p. 214.

[11]W. W. Abbot (ed.) Op. Cit., Vol. V, p. 304.

Allan Powell   63

a call to action, the Indians would precipitate confrontations with settlers when they tried to steal their horses. Then too, after receiving presents for services not yet given, the Indians would leave camp for their homes. These, and other practices created much hostility toward the Indians.

It is not difficult to find very negative opinions of Indians on the part of those who had to deal with their capricious habits. The following examples are used not only to illustrate the situation but to indicate the complexity of Christopher's task of recruiting. That he did remarkably well can be seen from the fact that he was called "Father" Gist by the Catawbas.[12]

Colonel Henry Bouquet, in a letter to Washington, reported from Raystown (Fort Bedford) that,

> "Our new comers Cherikee, are gone away after having Stolen our goods. It is a great humiliation for us to be obliged to Suffer the repeated Insolences of such Rascals; I think it would be easier to make Indians of our White men, than to coax that damned Tanny Race."[13]

Since time did not permit them, "to make Indians of our White men," the British had to depend upon the unpredictable services of Indians.

Washington's reply to Bouquet is a source of insight into Indian behavior. He wrote,

> "The Malbehavior of our Indians gives me great concern, if they were hearty in our Interest their services would be infinitly valuable; as I cannot conceive the best White men to be equal to them in the Woods but I fear they are too sensible of their high Importance to us, to render us any very acceptable Service."[14]

It would be naive to suppose that Indians were not "sensible of their high importance" and to act accordingly. They were certainly aware of Braddock's failure because he failed to attract enough support from the various Indian tribes.

Colonel John St. Clair, who had extensive dealings with the Indians, must have lost all patience with his uncertain allies. To Colonel Banquet he wrote, ". . . it is the greatest curse which Our Lord could pronounce against the greatest sinners, to have to do business with Indian friends . . . ."[15]

But Christopher's problems came from other sources as well. He had the delicate task of mediating between two governors who did not agree about the management of Indian affairs. On the one hand, Robert Dinwiddie, was an aggressive opponent of French expansion, who wanted ready access to southern Indians to assist in this mission. On the other was James Glen of South

---

[12]Kenneth P. Bailey, Christopher Gist, p. 148.

[13]S. K. Stevens, (ed. et. al.), The Papers of Henry Bouquet, Vol. II, p. 206.

[14]Ibid., p. 222.

[15]S. K. Stevens, (ed. et. al.) Op. Cit., Vol I. p. 405.

Carolina who made it clear that Indians from that source should be controlled by that colony.[16]

> "Relationships between Dinwiddie and Glen disintegrated so completely that by the time Gist became the Deputy Agent of Indian Affairs he could not at the same time be friendly to both. Glen was automatically in opposition to him because Gist represented Virginia."[17]

The consequence of this inter-Colonial friction was that Christopher's job of recruiting was made even more difficult and unpredictable. It was a near impossibility to know how many Indians would actually be available for service at any given point of time. Indians appeared and departed without giving service for the presents they had accepted as pay. At other times the expected presents were not on hand and the offended braves would turn about for their homes.

When there were mixups of any kind, the blame could be easily placed on Christopher's shoulders and he was assumed to have inflated the number of Indians he had recruited. As the campaign wore on and summer turned into fall, the number of Indians who left for home increased. The estimated 650 that were on hand in May was about 200 by July. By September had dwindled to less than 100.

When the French fort was evacuated in November, there were not very many Indians on hand. It would be difficult to determine whether the Forbes victory was helped more by the absence of western or "French" Indians or by the presence of "British" Indians. At one point, Colonel Bouquet expressed his exasperation at the shortage of Indians in a letter to General Forbes.

> "Gist's Catawbas and Cherokees exist only in his imagination and are reduced to twenty-eight Tuscaroras and Nantawayss, better fitted to carry off our presents than to fight. We must no longer count on any but ourselves.[18]

It seems manifestly unfair to hold Christopher accountable for the continual desertion on the part of the Indians. The campaign was slow getting started and it was a much longer than most campaigns of that day -- thus keeping the braves away from their homes for long periods of time.

Colonel Bouquet appears to be very suspicious of Christopher's claims about even those Indians that did appear. In a letter to General Forbes he reported that,

> "Captain Bullen with 31 Catawbas and 27 Tusc[aroras] are expected at Cumberland from Winchester. Some blankets are needed to outfit them, and especially some vermillion. Gist pretends that he has procured them [the Indians]. This is not very important, but he had no part in it."[19]

---

[16]Kenneth P. Bailey, Op. Cit., p. 120.

[17]Ibid., p. 121.

[18]S. K. Stevens, (ed. et. al.) Op. Cit., Vol. II, p. 217.

[19]Ibid., p. 356.

This is certainly an unwillingness to recognize the influence of Christopher as a supplier of Indian resources. Since it is known that Christopher was held in high esteem by the Indian tribes, it is clear that Colonel Bouquet did not have a similar assessment of his ability.

In retrospect, it would seem that the critics could have been more charitable when it is remembered that more Indians were on hand at all points in the Forbes Campaign than that led by Braddock. The Indian desertions did not alter the fact that Fort Duquesne was successfully taken.

With the conclusion of the Forbes-Bouquet expedition, Christopher continued his labors as Deputy of Indian Affairs with a primary interest in protecting the Virginia frontier. In addition, he was assigned the task of surveying land to be given to those veterans who had volunteered for Virginia's military forces. The bounty was the result of a proclamation issued in February, 1854, by Governor Dinwiddie. These lands were now open for settlement when the French evacuated the region.

As fate would have it, this was Christopher's last visit to the tract of land he had chosen for his permanent home. There is not much information about this period of his life. He must have been on horseback constantly - dividing his time between Virginia's frontier, the Carolina Indians and Williamsburg during the spring of 1759.[20]

On one of his visits to the Catawba nation during the summer of 1759, Christopher became infected with smallpox. The Catawba tribe was suffering from a severe epidemic which had played havoc with its population. The necessity of supervising the Indians on their journey to the western borders of Virginia made contact inevitable. Christopher succumbed to this frontier scourge at the age of 54 on July 25, 1759. He was not as fortunate as his friend and benefactor, George Washington, who had contracted the disease at an early age and had survived thus making his body immune to this dreaded disease.

At an earlier period there had been some debate about the place and time of Christopher's death. A prominent writer had stated that Christopher had died somewhere in Georgia or South Carolina. But more recent evidence makes it fairly certain about the circumstances of his death. A letter from Captain John Tulleken has the following terse announcement.

> "I thought it proper to advise you that Capt Gist Deputy Agent for Indian Affairs here [Winchester], died on the Road from Williamsburg 25th instant with the Small Pox. This I mention, that if the General expects any Indians, some Person be ordered by him to take the Direction of them, Otherwise they Cant be Supplied with Necessaries."[21]

There are other documents which give authority to the foregoing claim, making it unnecessary to carry on the debate. An indefatigable servant of colony and crown had been brought down before the final victory over the French. Some might argue that he deserved to have been spared long enough

---

[20]It is a rather fascinating footnote in history that one of the businesses with whom Christopher is almost certain to have conducted business is still in operation in the restored historic section of Williamsburg. The reader may now visit William Prentis & Co. on Duke of Gloucester Street for a view of a general store of the colonial period.

[21]Donald H. Kent (ed. et. al.), Op. Cit., Vol. III, P. 468.

to be a witness to the victories at Quebec and Montreal. But this was not to be.

The scant details of Christopher's last days seems to indicate a continuation of conditions which haunted him throughout his adult life. Creditors were still pressing relentlessly for payment of bills. Colonel John St. Clair wrote to General Amherst about his experience in closing out Christopher's accounts in Winchester.

> "I shall not dispute but there are small sums due to the Inhabitants of Winchester, but in the present Situation of these accounts it is impossible for us to distinguish which are just. I know that Mr. Gists Credit was so bad that I was obliged to pass my word at one of the Shops at Winchester for some goods at that time, which I have since seen paid."[22]

But the financial accounts which appear to put Christopher in a bad light must be set against the total picture. If this be allowed, Christopher would be a credit to any canvas. Blemishes are there to be sure - but these fade into obscurity when compared to the many exploits which make the name of Christopher Gist a standout in frontier history.

---

[22]Kenneth P. Bailey, Op. Cit., p. 151.

Chapter VIII

The Legacy of Christopher Gist

It would be an easier task to give an adequate report on one who left a more complete record of their achievements. Three short journals and a hand full of letters are meager fare as a basis to use for a portrait of a life so eventful as that of our subject. History would have been better served if Christopher had indulged in more self promotion. On one of his many trips to Williamsburg, he might have visited an artist to paint an heroic portrait in the colorful garb of a ranger or scout. But this seems to be out of character for the trail-wise explorer.

Again, if Christopher had been driven by an inner urge to write of his many exploits the world would be richer for his efforts. But he was a man of action and it is to others that we are indebted for other fragments about his unceasing travels. Possibly Christopher and Washington between them traversed more frontier trails and packhorse woods than any other colonial travelers of their time.

It is evident from what is known that Christopher was unusually strong and courageous. He was possessed of a strong will and a body that was seemingly unaffected by pain. Long, lonely trails, frozen streams, biting cold winds, hostile or uncertain Indians and frontier diseases failed to thwart his urge to cover new ground. Christopher took all in stride and met the demands of each situation as they arose.

To have acquired the skills of a surveyor, explorer, trader, negotiator, diplomat and soldier-scout was a remarkable accomplishment, exhibiting considerable versatility. Putting his earlier catastrophic losses behind him, Christopher doggedly struggled to improve his lot as he looked for better days ahead - days which continually eluded him.

Some would argue that the proper person to receive whatever praises to be given should have been Sarah, his wife, who almost alone struggled heroically to raise five children in rustic cabins on a dangerous frontier. The point is well taken but must be weighed against the way scouts earned their livelihood. the boys apparently did not resent their father for his chronic absenteeism because they sometimes traveled with him and served under him in the Virginia forces.

The family was further scattered upon the death of Sarah Gist. One daughter, Ann, lived at the William Fairfax estate at Belvoir for a period of time.[1] She has been rumored to have been on intimate terms with young George Washington. She was in her early twenties when Washington (also in

---

[1] Kenneth P. Bailey, Christopher Gist, p. 171.

his early twenties) came to Wills Creek in 1753. It will be recalled that Washington was also a frequent visitor to the Fairfax home.

It has been asserted that," Her [Ann's] first known suitor was George Washington.:[2] This has been further embellished. "later, among the men who visited her father, none was more attractive than George. Although it was a match that could not be, it lasted long enough for George to write a love letter or two."[3] The source of this claim avers that Mrs. Washington destroyed these letters.[4]

Returning to Christopher and the impact of his life we are not amiss to include a short, romanticized (and some would say suspect) tribute to the great trail blazer. The author of the Horn Papers is most generous. He writes,

> "Christopher Gist knew the Mohongalo Valley and upper Ohio River borders more than any white man in his day, and with Joshua (Bowlegs) knew every Indian trail from the Sus de La Hanna to the Ohio before the Old French and Indian War. Being of a sound mind, and a tall but lithe body, he could travel fast and long in duration never giving much thought to himself, but much care to his mules. He feared no man or animal, sharp in expression of feature, strong in his likes and dislikes. He would kill on enemy without a minutes warning, but would share his Virginia tobacco with all his friends."[5]

Since the Horn Papers are not considered reliable, the reader might take a portion of salt with the foregoing account.

One important element in the legacy of Christopher Gist is to be found in the conduct of his sons after his death. After having served the Crown faithfully and with valor during the French and Indians War, two sons, Nathaniel and Richard changed their loyalties and fought with the colonial forces against England. Christopher, had he lived, would have been too old to fight in that contest but it is likely that he too would have turned against the King and would have served with his friend, George Washington.

Nathaniel, after some delay, ". . . joined the Virginia militia and on January 11, 1777, Washington appointed him colonel to raise a regiment of rangers in Virginia. In 1780 he was taken prisoner by the British at Charleston, but he was released on January 1, 1781; and he then retired from the army."[6] Nathaniel along with many other British subjects made the move for independence.

Richard was killed at the battle of King's Mountain[7] - thus making the supreme sacrifice for the cause of independence. What influences were behind these changes of allegiance? It is reasonable to assume that the Gist family

---

[2] Ibid., p. 171.

[3] Ibid., p. 171.

[4] Ibid., p. 171.

[5] See Ibid., pp. 194-5.

[6] Lawrence A. Orrill, Op. Cit., p. 217.

[7] Ibid., p. 218.

first regarded the French as a threat and resisted their encroachments by resort to arms. It is no less reasonable to assume that contact with the British military establishment during the war and then being a witness to British colonial policies in the post war period they again perceived a threat and again took up arms.

It is a remarkable historical fact, overlooked by many, that only thirteen years separated the Peace of Paris of 1763 and the Declaration of Independence in 1776. It took seven years of war to win North America and only thirteen to lose it. This can be only partly explained by proofs of maladministration on the part of the British. It must be supplemented by proofs of the growth of a spirit of independence on this side of the Atlantic.

What many students of American history remember are the vexing tax and regulatory policies which the British government pursued during the post war period - policies which alienated their colonial subjects. But it would be instructive to take a cursory review of the friction-creating situations that developed before and during the French and Indian War which incubated the attitudes toward independence long before Grenville, Townshend and others completed the process of alienation.

Douglas Edward Leach, in Roots of Conflict, has provided an impressive list of events which served to drive a wedge between the colonies and England. Several of them are deserving of attention. To begin, there was widespread profiteering throughout the colonies which inevitably added to the cost of the war. More detestable was the outright sale of goods to the enemy.

British officers were at times forced to threaten the inhabitants for the use of their wagons to move the army westward. General Thomas Gage claimed that it was the delay in getting wagon teams and the insufficient number collected which brought about the defeat of Braddock at the Monongahela.[8]

There were also shortages of troops to fight the French. As the war lingered on, British recruiters would entice indentured servants and apprentices to leave their work places for the army, thus placing a financial loss on their masters. At the same time, troops were forced upon the civilian population when there was a shortage of quarters. Forced quartering created much resentment against England. Int he winter of 1756-57 some 146 officers and 1,448 enlisted men were forced upon the unhappy town of Albany.[9]

A bitter pill to swallow for colonial officers was the ranking system used in the British army. Even before war was declared, a proclamation from London declared that,

". . . it is Our Will and Pleasure that all troops serving by Commission signed Us, or by Our General Commanding in Chief in North America; shall take Rank before all Troops which may serve by Commission from any of the Governors. . . ."[10]

---

[8]Douglas Edward Leach, Roots of Conflict, p. 82.

[9]Ibid., p. 91.

[10]Ibid., p. 119.

By this order, a provincial captain would be outranked by a British regular captain, This, of course, was regarded as an insult by colonial officers and as another instance of their usual haughtiness. It was particularly resented by George Washington who resigned his commission in Virginia for a period of time. It is most unlikely that the Gists saw the situation any differently.

British officers did not disguise their low opinion of Americans. Their correspondence reveals a generous portion of denunciation of American characteristics. Without quoting the many available passages, it will be sufficient to list the typical adjectives used. These include: slothful, ignorant, indolent, undependable, obstinate, ungovernable, cowardly dogs, scum and that they were unfit for military service, good for nothing and vagabonds.[11] It would be both naive and unwise to suggest that these attitudes had no effect on the colonial population.

The impressment of American citizens into the British navy was yet another source of friction. Conditions on board British vessels were inhuman - resulting in large numbers of desertions. In order to fill vacant berths, captains in the British navy would send press gangs into American seaport towns to kidnap the unwary or board a merchant transport and forcibly take the needed number of able-bodied seamen. Needless to report, resentment ran high.

One final source of conflict (there is no need to multiply instances) which stimulated the urge to independence was the Proclamation of 1763. By this order, white settlement west of the Alleghany mountains was forbidden. Also, colonial traders were required to get a license from London before they could engage in business with Indians. This well-intended attempt to reduce friction between Indians and whites actually created more hostility and in the end failed to achieve its objective. It failed because of the,

> ". . . sudden intrusion of a new force, a force whose imminent rise could not have been forseen in 1763 because its first faint stirrings were not yet apparent. Then, within the brief lapse of three years, there came the transition. The great change was brought about by the mysterious and unheralded materialization on the border scene of men and women of a sort hitherto unknown, The Frontier People"[12]

These were the people who saw the unsettled lands to the west as a place of opportunity and hope and who were not to be permanently dissuaded from acquiring these lands.

But there was yet another class of people who had an eye on these lands - the speculators - and this class included some very important Americans. Between the land hungry frontiersmen, the veterans who had been promised land for military service and the speculators there was little chance that a proclamation from London would effectively contain their westward advance.

It must be recalled that the Gist Settlement near Uniontown was in the forbidden area of settlement. Further, the sons of Christopher Gist were due lands in the area for their service. This order would, without doubt, be seen as another unfair, repressive policy to be looked at with contempt.

---

[11] Ibid., pp. 130-132.

[12] Dale Van Every, Forth To The Wilderness, p. 23.

Washington's opinion of this order is probably typical of his day. He wrote to William Crawford, his land agent, that,

> "I can never look upon that proclamation in any other light (but this I say between ourselves) than a temporary expedient to quiet the minds of the Indians. . .Any person, therefore, who neglects the present opportunity of hunting out good lands, and in some measure marking and distinguishing them for his own, in order to keep others from settling the, will never regain it."[13]

It is clear, then, that Washington as a member of the Ohio Company and thus a speculator had no intention of standing idly by and letting this land become the property of others.

Simultaneously with all the foregoing events which had a cumulative impact on the colonial psyche was another idea which was to ferment until it produced devastating consequences. This idea is well summed up by Leach. He writes,

> "The staggering defeat suffered by General Edward Braddock's army in 1755 had released in the colonies a heady idea that some American provincials had been secretly nourishing. This was that Americans through long experience in fighting both the stealthy Indians and the shrewd French in a wilderness environment, had acquired a special expertise in wilderness warfare that was neither possessed nor appreciated by the regulars. This idea lead slowly but inexorably to another, even more heady -that under certain favorable conditions a small force of well-armed and woods-wise colonists could rout a much larger, more ponderous formation of professional European soldiers. It was an intriguing proposition, not easily forgotten.[14]

Christopher and his sons were observers and participants in the events we have described. They were both the creators and carriers of frontier attitudes, values and practices which shaped American destiny during the war and then in the post-war era.

They were nurtured on the myths of self sufficiency and unfettered movement which figured greatly in the movement for independence. We are deeply indebted to them for their tenacity against the French, their energy in clearing the way for settlement of the transmontane region and for their sacrifices in securing our independence from England. This is a legacy unrivaled among free people of any age. Christopher Gist exemplifies this independent restless spirit. He contributed greatly to independence and westward expansion and as a consequence deserves a place in history on a footing with the more famous frontiersmen such as Boone, Kenton, Croghan and Cresap.

---

[13]Ibid., pp. 269-70.

[14]Douglas Edward Leach, Op. Cit., p. 165.

Appendix

An almost angelic Washington is saved by Gist when ice jars the rough-hewn raft and the youthful Washington is thrown into the frigid Allegheny. This is one artistic version of this event. They spent the night on an island in the river - a night so cold that Gist was frost bitten.

This is another attempt to portray the dangerous crossing of the Alleghany river on December 29, 1753. While Gist and Washington make very little of the incident, others have claimed that it was the second time in two days that Gist saved Washington's life.

Gist (left) and Washington escape death when an Indian guide suddenly turns on them and fires his gun at close range. The account of this near disaster on December 27, 1753 is also recorded in the journals of both men.

This is still another portrayal of the attempt to shoot either Gist or Washington enroute from Fort Le Boeuf. Gist wrestles the luckless assassin to the ground, thus preventing a second shot. He avers that he would have killed him but was prevented by orders from Washington.

This is a letter written by Gist to George Washington from Philadelphia on November 1. The typed version is on the following page. It should be observed that Gist has good penmanship and shows evidence of an education beyond that associated with a frontier scout.

My dear Friend   Philadelphia Nov 1st 1755

I have taken all the pains in my Power to find the true intents of the Indians. Monnacatootha is returned from the Six Nations, but is not yet come from Shamokin but I understand he and the Other Chiefs will on Sunday or Monday be at John Harrises Ferry where I intend God willing to meet them. but I am to go to Conrad Wiser and get all he knows; I have the governor's Letters to him on that Head, so I shall be Able to give you all the Intelligence that can possibly be got. The Governor Morris last night Offer'd me a Capt's commission in this province not Knowing I had one under you. I find By that they Intend to do Something in Ernest The Two Lower County's have Passed the Militia Law and Offers   2000 the Governor has wrote you by express - I will be with you or Send an Express when I am Rightly certain of the Indians Intentions pay Excuse hast

                              Sir Most Humb. Servt:
                              Christ: Gist

This is a letter written to George Washington from Lancaster, Pennsylvania by Christopher Gist. A typed account is on the following page. In spite of being broke, Christopher is very successful at recruiting troops.

Dear Sir   Lancaster Town Pennsylvania, Nov 24th 1755

    I have Sent twenty of My Şoldiers to York Town, who are all in good Sperritts There and Two I now send to them. Tomorrow I shall follow them I have been forced to Borrow money, and if I could have had money enough I believe I should have had 50 men by This Time. I hope I Shall be properly Supplyd with cash to answer what I have done and if we want men I think I can Soon get them. We have had no Scalping work hear this Week. We have a flying Story of 7000 French Going to Attack Gen l Johnston which hope is not true. I shall be at Winchester with all Possible Speed in Ye Intrum I am

P. S. Diter Giles is   Sir Yr Most Hum. Servt,
      with me   Christ: Gist
      with whom
      Company hope
      you'l be pleased

        C. G.

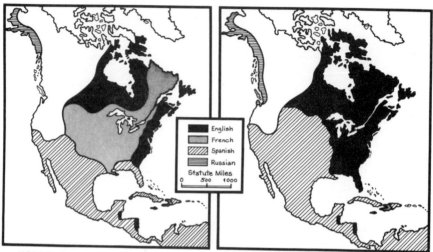

NORTH AMERICA BEFORE 1763   NORTH AMERICA AFTER 1763

The vast territory shown on the left map (French) was ceded to England as a consequence of England's victory after the French and Indian War.

Bibliography

Abbot, W. W. (ed.), The Papers of George Washington. Vols. 1-6 Charlottesville: University Press of Virginia, 1983.

Backstruck, Lloyd De Witt, Virginia's Colonial Soldiers. Baltimore: Genealogy Publishing Co., 1988.

Bailey, Kenneth P., Christopher Gist. Hamden: The Shoe string Press, Inc., 1976.

Bradley, A. G., The Fight With France For North America. Landon: Archibald Constable & Co., LTD, 1908.

Brown, Stuart E. Jr., Virginia Baron: The Story of Thomas 6th Lord Fairfax. Berryville: Chesapeake Book Co., 1965.

Brown, William Hand (ed.) Correspondence of Governor Horatio Sharpe. Vol. I Baltimore: Maryland Historical Society, 1888.

Darlington, William M., Christopher Gist's Journals. Pittsburgh: J. R. Weldin & Co., 1893.

Dorsey, Jean Muir & Dorsey, Maxwell J, Christopher Gist of Maryland and Some of His Descendants 1679-1957. Chicago: John S. Swift Co., Inc., 1958.

Eckert, Allan W., The Conquerors. New York: Bantam Books, 1970.

Eckert, Allan W., Wilderness Empire. New York: Bantam Books, 1969.

Every, Dale Van, Forth To The Wilderness. New York: William Morrow and Co., 1961.

Freeman, Douglas Southall, George Washington Vols. 1 & 2, New York: Charles Scribner's Sons, 1948.

Gee, Wilson, The Gist Family of South Carolina and Its Maryland Antecedents. Charlottesville: Jarman's Inc., 1934.

Hanna, Charles A., The Wilderness Trail. New York: G. P. Putnam's Sons, 1911.

Johnson, Allen and Malone, Dumas, Dictionary of American Biography. New York: Charles Scribner's Sons, 1931.

Kopperman, Paul E., Braddock at The Monongahela. Pittsburgh: University of Pittsburgh Press, 1977.

Leach, Douglas Edward, Roots of Conflict. Chapel Hill: The University of North Carolina Press, 1986.

Lowdermilk, Will H., History of Cumberland, Maryland. Baltimore: Regional Publishing Co., 1971.

McCardell, Lee, Ill Starred General. Pittsburgh: University of Pittsburgh Press, 1958.

Mulkearn, Lois, George Mercer Papers. Pittsburgh: University of Pittsburgh Press, 1954.

O'Meara, Walter, Guns at The Forks. Pittsburgh: University of Pittsburgh Press, 1979.

Parkman, Francis, Moncalm and Wolfe. New York: Atheneum, 1984.

Parkman, Francis, The Conspiracy of Pontiac. Boston: Little, Brown, and Co., 1899.

Sargent, Winthrop, The History of an Expedition Against Fort Du Quesne, Under Major - General Edward Braddock. Philadelphia: Lippencott, Grambo & Co., 1855.

Stevens, S. K. and Kent, Donald H. (eds.), The Papers of Henry Bouquet. Vols. 1-4, The Pennsylvania Historical and Museum Commission, 1951.

Vogt, Helen, Westward of Ye Laurall Hills. Parsons: McClain Printing Co., 1976.

Washington, George, The Journal of Major George Washington. Williamsburg: Colonial Williamsburg Foundation, 1959.

Journals

Clark, Russel S., "Christopher Gist," The Papers of the Christopher Gist Historical Society, Vol. I. 1950-51.

Giddens, Paul H., "The French and Indian War in Maryland," Maryland Historical Magazine, Vol. XXX, December, 1935.

Johnston, Christopher, "Gist Family of baltimore County," Maryland Historical Magazine, Vol. VIII #4, December, 1913.

Orrvill, Lawrence A., "Christopher Gist and His Sons, " Western Pennsylvania Historical Magazine, Vol. 15, 1932.

Trimble, David B., "Christopher Gist and Settlement on the Monongahela, 1752-1754," Virginia Magazine of History and Biography, Vol. 63, January, 1955.

Other Books by Allan Powell:

Fort Frederick: Potomac Outpost
Fort Cumberland
Fort Loudoun: Winchester's Defense in the French and
                  Indian War

From Seminary to Skepticism

41 years -   Educator - Professor, Philosophy and Sociology -
             Hagerstown Junior College

Member -   American Philosophical Association

Author -   Many Articles, International Torch

Columnist - Contributing Columnist, Hagerstown Sunday Herald